WE SAID

THEY SAID

50 THINGS
**Parents and Teachers of
Students with Autism
Want Each Other to Know**

Cassie Zupke

We Said, They Said:

50 Things Parents and Teachers of Students with Autism Want Each Other to Know

All marketing and publishing rights guaranteed to and reserved by:

FUTURE HORIZONS INC.

721 W. Abram Street

Arlington, TX 76013

800•489•0727

817•277•0727

817•277•2270 (fax)

E-mail: *info@fhautism.com*

www.fhautism.com

ISBN: 978-1-935274-86-5

DEDICATION

To my husband. Without his support, this book would never have been written.

To my children, who ate a lot of frozen pizza while I wrote it.

And to the rest of my family, who never once told me that cooking dinner was more important than writing.

ACKNOWLEDGMENTS

I'd like to take this opportunity to acknowledge a very special group of people. The parents of children with difficulties often work very hard on their behalf. We have to—they're our kids. It's our job to help them to the best of our ability. But, there are also a lot of people who have chosen to help our children—just because they want to.

There are teachers who go far above and beyond what's mandated by law, who work very hard to help our kids succeed. There are administrators who research and create special programs because they will help our kids reach new heights. Experts specialize in autism and other special needs because they really want to help children. Members of all kinds of community groups don't have to include our kids, but they do anyway, because it's the right thing to do. There are students who help the child next to them who is struggling and is frankly more than a little odd. Friends and neighbors may not have a clue why our kids do what they do, but they invite them over to play anyway. Volunteers give their own time and money to help other people's kids, just because they care about them. People like these have touched my life and the lives of those in my family in more ways than they'll ever know. My son's life is better because of them—and so is mine. They've inspired me and led me forward during the times I didn't know which way to turn. They are angels on earth, and I am in their debt in more ways than I can ever repay.

CONTENTS

introduction _____ ix

25 Things Parents of Children with Autism Want Teachers to Know   xvii

1. Listen to Me _____ 1
2. I Didn't Cause My Child's Autism _____ 9
3. Typical Parenting Skills Are Not Enough_____ 13
4. I Have No One to Guide Me _____ 19
5. Hooey _____ 25
6. Social Rejection _____ 31
7. Giving Me Advice _____ 37
8. My Goals for My Child_____ 43
9. My Child's Developmental Path _____ 47
10. The Grieving Process _____ 53
11. Hope and Delusions _____ 57
12. Acceptance and Realism _____ 61
13. My Options _____ 65
14. Dealing with Transitions _____ 69
15. Childhood Development _____ 73
16. What Are We Doing? _____ 77
17. Your Challenges_____ 83
18. Can I Trust You? _____ 87
19. I Need to Prove Myself_____ 93
20. Social Interaction May Be Difficult for Me _____ 99
21. Why Sometimes I Don't Try _____ 109
22. I'm Tired_____ 115
23. I Am Afraid _____ 123
24. Don't Give Up on Us _____ 127
25. I Love My Child _____ 131

CONTENTS

25 Things Teachers of Children with Autism Want Parents to Know   135

1. I Care about Your Child _____ 137
2. Autism May Be New to Me _____ 143
3. Teaching Methods _____ 147
4. Your Child's Privacy _____ 151
5. The Other Students in My Class _____ 155
6. Can I Trust You? _____ 159
7. What Kind of Parent Are You?_____ 165
8. Yelling Never Works _____ 169
9. Legal Help _____ 173
10. Services, Accommodations, and Modifications _____ 179
11. I Don't Have A Magic Wand _____ 185
12. Assessing Your Child's Progress_____ 189
13. Why I Tell You Things You Don't Want to Hear _____ 195
14. Realism and Acceptance _____ 199
15. Teaching Independence _____ 203
16. Special Education Is Changing _____ 209
17. Living, Vocational, and Social Skills _____ 213
18. The Future _____ 219
19. If You Have Questions, Ask Me_____ 223
20. Homework _____ 229
21. Consultations_____ 237
22. What You Model at Home _____ 243
23. Funding_____ 249
24. Medicating Your Child _____ 255
25. Get to Know Us_____ 259

Conclusion _____ 265

About the Author _____ 269

INTRODUCTION

In my role as the founder and director of a non-profit organization that provides education and support for students with mild autism, as well as their parents and educators, I've talked to a lot of people. I've been a mentor and a trainer. I've attended meetings, given presentations, reassured parents and teachers, advocated for children, helped to dry tears, and offered more advice than was probably wanted. I've initiated programs and later thrown some of them out to build better ones. Over the years, I've worked with hundreds of families and educators. This book represents the summation of what they've talked to me about—their fears, their concerns, and their passions—the things that drive them when they sit down at the meeting table and decide how they're going to help a child.

These are the things they argue about.

Often, these issues are not mentioned in meetings. They are feelings that are discussed only among other parents or only between teachers. Some of the feelings are private. We would never admit them out loud for fear of the judgments that would come down on us. Some of them are buried so deep within us that we don't even know we have them, even though they show in our actions and in the stories we tell.

This book is not a manual about how parents and teachers should be. It's about how we are—our faults and frailties, along with our strengths and passions. Should we feel the way we sometimes feel? No, but we do anyway. It's human nature. The sooner we learn to accept the way we are, the sooner we can get past our conflicts to help our children.

In this book, I assume that everyone involved—parents, teachers, and administrators—are compassionate, skilled, and rational people who are working for the benefit of the child. You and I know that's not always the case. Most people are wonderful and dedicated to helping the children in their care, but there are a handful of folks out there who aren't really up to the job. They may not have good coping skills, they may not care about children, they may be downright mean, or they may have challenges of their own. These people are rare, but they're around.

All the books in the world won't change that, and, unfortunately, mine won't either. But, this book does explain why many people do what they do when they're put in the situation of having to raise or teach a child with special needs. I hope it provides the information you need the next time you're looking for a way to help a child you care about.

Since this book is a distillation of what hundreds of parents and teachers have discussed with me, it describes emotions that most of us feel at one time or another. None of us feels all of these things all the time. I don't know how we'd make it if we did. Each of us has faced and overcome some of these issues, and circumstances may force us to face them again. The best thing we can do is to hold hands and help each other through the hard times.

The people I've worked with care for children with autism, but their stories are common to most special-needs families and their teachers. Raising and teaching kids with special needs can be difficult. It can be stressful, frustrating, and very isolating. It feels like there is never enough information or support. The fact that we care so much for our children makes our struggles more profound, but when we succeed, it makes our children's victories so much sweeter. Our kids are worth it.

If you are reading this book and you have autism, please know that children do not cause the feelings parents and teachers express here. As parents and educators, we care about our kids. It's what we do. We especially want to help our children with anything that makes their lives more difficult. If it's something we can "fix," okay. If it feels like we can't fix it, we don't like it. The bigger the problems, the more we want to be able to fix them.

We don't dislike autism, and we don't dislike our children because they have autism. We are concerned for our children's futures and how autism will affect their lives. If we knew today that they would be able to overcome the challenges that autism brings, we would accept autism as easily as we accept our child's hair color. But right now, we don't know that. So we worry, and we feel guilty because we can't make the difficulties go away. That's just the way we are.

Autism is a spectrum disorder, meaning it affects different people to different degrees. Medical and mental health professionals have divided the diagnosis of autism into several "subtypes," such as high-functioning autism, Rett syndrome, pervasive developmental disorder—not otherwise specified, childhood disintegrative disorder, and classic autism, which is sometimes further subdivided into mild, moderate, or severe categories. Being able to group folks with autism according to the type and severity of their symptoms is helpful to professionals but can sometimes leave parents steaming. Parents may feel that the labels given to their child gloss over their child's unique qualities and could lead educators and medical professionals to treat the label and not the child.

Some people also think that parents who use the term *high-functioning autism* are saying that their children are "better" than children who are more severely affected by autism. However, that's generally not the case. Parents say their child has *high-functioning autism* because this term best describes the particular set of difficulties their child has. *Severe autism, moderate autism, mild autism,* and *high-functioning autism* may be broad, poorly defined terms, but they give everyone who is familiar with autism a quick snapshot of the types of difficulties and needs that affect the person they describe.

In this book, I use the term *autism* broadly, but I am very selective in my choice of pronouns. Here, I refer to kids as "he" and teachers as "she," and the parents I talk about are typically moms. I did this for the sake of simplicity and clarity. It just gets too confusing to have too many pronouns floating around. I know there are many girls with autism. Autism in girls often goes undiagnosed or is underdiagnosed because girls are better than boys at mimicking social interaction. As our knowledge about autism increases, hopefully we'll learn more about how to identify the needs of our girls and how to best help them, too. Also, I know there are many wonderful male teachers out there and a whole lot of very involved dads. Good for you. You're just as important in our children's lives as their female role models. I'm not trying to ignore you or imply that you are less important in any way. I'm just attempting to make this book easier to read.

There are going to be some parents who strongly disagree with some of the things I've written from the teacher's point of view. While most parents of kids with special needs have been treated fairly by the personnel at their school, frankly, there are some who haven't. Those parents tend to have an unfavorable view of teachers and school districts. I can't blame them. I also can't blame teachers who have been verbally or physically assaulted by parents, if they're a little skeptical of what I've written from the parent's viewpoint. That's okay. Everyone has had his or her own experiences, and I'm not doubting any of them.

What I've written here reflects the views and attitudes of the majority of parents and teachers I have dealt with. No matter what you hear in the school's parking lot or lunchroom, remember that unhappy people tend to talk the loudest, and happy people tend to stay quiet. The people you hear from are the ones with complaints. The opinions of people who are content often go unheard until you ask.

It took me several years to gather the information necessary to write this book—and a while longer to figure out how to present it so that it is useful. I hope I've succeeded, and I hope you find something here that makes your next parent-teacher conference go more smoothly.

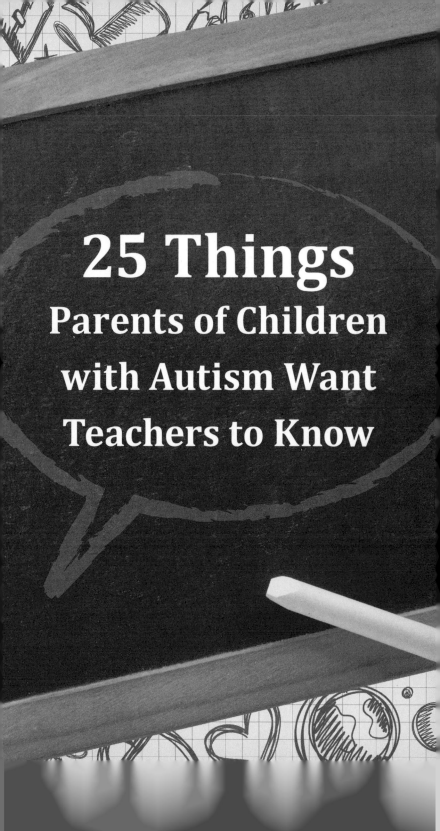

25 Things
Parents of Children with Autism Want Teachers to Know

1

LISTEN TO ME

My child and I have not had easy lives. Since the day my son was born, I've had to fight to keep him safe. Not only have I done all the things for him that parents of typically developing children do—fed him, clothed him, given him shelter, and taught him as he has grown—but I've also had to deal with the fact that he lives in a world where he does not fit in—a world that doesn't understand his needs.

I've always had to think ahead, assess new situations, and try to figure out everything that could go wrong before it happened. He has as much intelligence as other kids, but not their common sense, so it's been hard just keeping him alive.

His impulsivity has been a nightmare. When he was little, he ran. If my hand wasn't somewhere on his body to keep him with me, he was gone. Nothing I said made him slow down, much less come back. To get him to stop, I had to physically run and catch him, every time he got away. Any time we left the house, he had to be strapped into his car seat or stroller, or I had to hold onto him. Otherwise, he would run the instant my back was turned. I've fished him out of deep water, and I've chased him through shopping malls and parking lots as I prayed for his safety. I've snatched him away from unfriendly animals and pulled him down from high places. Locked doors and windows couldn't keep him in the house, once he learned to pull chairs over and stand on them to reach the locks. More than once I've had to chase him down the street.

Coping with his sensory difficulties has given me more than a few gray hairs. Things other children enjoyed drove him nuts. Balloons terrified him because they might pop. He would cry in pain at movie theaters because the sound was so loud. Eating mashed potatoes at Thanksgiving made him gag and vomit. The seams on his socks hurt him, and the neck openings on his shirts choked him. He could only wear pants with elastic waistbands, because other kinds of pants felt too tight, and they could only be blue, because "that's the color pants are supposed to be." The smell of cigarettes made him sick, and he made sure the person smoking knew it. Cat fur felt really good to him, so he petted every cat he could get his hands on, whether the animal liked it or not. He also liked the hair of the little girl who lived next door, except she screamed when he pulled it—which made him laugh. Her mother didn't find it so funny.

I've had to run social interference since he was a baby. His grandparents asked why he acted the way he did—none of the other grandchildren behaved this way. The kids at the park wanted to know the same thing. Their mothers didn't care why he did what he did—they just didn't want him doing it near their children. When one of my son's classmates invited him to his birthday party (because his mother insisted), my boy really wanted to go. The entire time we were there, I stayed within an arm's length to make sure he didn't break something, or open the presents, or eat the cake before it was served, or insult someone, or take his pants off because they itched, or do something else I couldn't anticipate. The other mothers were very kind, but in some ways their compassion seemed to magnify the fact that my son was so far behind developmentally, which made me feel even worse. I was so relieved when we had to leave early.

I've spent years worrying about how my child will make it as an adult when I can no longer help him. Will he be able to work? Or live independently? Will he be able to keep himself safe from predators, bankruptcy, legal entanglements, and loneliness? Who will love him when I'm gone? I've searched for answers. What can we do now—what can we teach him so he can function independently one day? I've read books and attended conferences, searched out gurus, changed our diet, and had to learn more about psychotropic drugs than any parent should have to. I've taken him to neurologists, psychiatrists, psychologists, gastroenterologists, alternative-medicine doctors, karate class, and soccer, and done more hours at the homework table than I can count. We've made progress, but I'm still scared he won't learn everything he needs to know.

Since the day he was born, I've had to be constantly vigilant. It hasn't been easy, and I'm not done yet. We've got a lot of progress to make in just a few short years.

Now he's coming into your classroom, and you're asking me to hand that responsibility over to you.

After all we've been through, I'm expected to give him over to someone I don't know. I'm supposed to trust you to keep him safe and meet his needs, even though he may act like no other child you've ever had in your classroom, and even though you may not have had any training in autism. I'm meant to believe that you will somehow like him and care about him, even though he may be more work and cause you more grief than all the rest of your students put together.

That's asking a lot from me.

You'll be making many decisions that will affect his life now and maybe forever—decisions I have no control over. It will be up to you to decide how much you learn about autism and how you apply that knowledge. Your attitude and behavior will help decide whether his classmates are helpful and friendly or mean and rejecting. You'll choose how much time and attention you give him in the classroom and how nice you'll be. These choices are ones you'll make yourself, and there's not much I can do to influence them.

There are also choices we're supposed to make as a team. Big choices—like Individualized Education Program (IEP) types of things. What supports and modifications will he get? How much homework and class work will he do? Will he get speech services, social-skills training, or adapted physical education (PE) classes? How about occupational therapy or counseling? What are his goals and objectives? What are his biggest difficulties, and how can we help him overcome them?

Together, we're supposed to chart his path. That's what an IEP is all about—a team making a plan for how we're going to proceed. But sometimes, that's not the way it works. I sit down at the table and spend the next 2 hours looking at data you've accumulated and listening to the goals you've already decided. Then you hand me a pen and ask me to finalize the paperwork—my only contribution to our plan. Where was the part when you asked for my input? When did you ask me about my knowledge of my child, my goals and expectations, my ability to work with him at home, our struggles, and our progress? My concerns and fears—when did you ask for those?

Sometimes I have put my foot down. I've stopped the flow of the meeting to try to make sure you understand my perspective. Sometimes you listen and accept what I say, but sometimes you just shake your head and say, "That's not what we see at school." Solutions I bring forward are met with,

"That's just not practical," or "We can't do that," or "Please be realistic."

Our perspectives are different, formed in different situations, with different expectations and goals. So are our resources and skills. But my viewpoint is just as valid as yours, even if we disagree. If you don't take the time to listen to me and forge a plan we can both live with, it won't matter how good your plan is. It won't work well. The things you do at school will be undone at home, just as my work will be undone when he goes back the next day. Any progress you make wouldn't be half of what it could have been, if we had worked together.

He is not your child. He is mine. When he is finished with school, you'll hand him back over to me, and he and I are going to have to live with whatever we've accomplished. So although I will share some of the decision-making with you while he is in your care, don't expect me to give it over to you completely.

You wouldn't let someone else decide your child's fate. Neither will I.

2

I DIDN'T CAUSE MY CHILD'S AUTISM

t's not my fault my child has autism. When I was pregnant, I didn't drink or do drugs. I didn't ride roller coasters or swing on trapezes or stay up too late at night. I didn't marry a man who was a druggie and whose sperm swam crooked. After my child was born, I didn't neglect him. I played with him and responded to him and laughed and smiled and fed him well and let him watch only a little more TV than he should have. I loved my baby and did all the things that mothers of typically developing children do. But my child turned out to be autistic, and theirs didn't.

We didn't decide to have a child with autism. When my husband and I lay in bed at night dreaming of our angel-to-be, we didn't envision a sweet,

wonderful little whirlwind of a child who would get kicked out of preschool twice before he turned 3 years old. We didn't encourage him to obsess over his toys or show him how to line them up in perfect rows or teach him that it was okay to ignore Grandma even though she'd traveled more than 1,000 miles to see him. We disciplined him, and still he took our house apart piece by piece. We taught him not to hit other kids, and still he did it far longer than typically developing toddlers do. We made him ask for things before we gave them to him, and his language was still delayed and garbled. Our son developed autism, and no matter what we do, we can't change that fact.

Why does my child have autism, and yours doesn't? Genetics could play a part. We spun the wheel of chance and received a bundle of joy that came up beautiful, intelligent, and autistic. You spun the wheel and hit a different combination. Environmental factors play their role too, but my son's physical and emotional environment wasn't so different from that of your child. What made mine autistic and yours not? As of right now, no one knows.

When my husband and I decided to have a baby, we didn't know we were making a decision that would radically change our lives forever. While every baby changes the lives of his parents, having a child with special needs launches you onto another planet, with no way back to your old world. Ever. For some parents, this can mean changing diapers well into their 80s. It may mean living the rest of their lives with someone who is angry, anxious, violent, or depressed. It does mean entering a world of isolation, where few of your friends and family understand your child and why you do what you do. It may mean giving up your career and your education, because you can't find anyone else who can care for your child. It can mean designating an unexpectedly large portion of your income to therapies, tutoring, doctor visits, and medicines, because they don't come cheap. Your other children will get less attention and time, and so will your marriage.

We didn't decide to have a child with autism, and we did nothing to cause it. You could have had him as easily as I did. But, the thought of that makes me sad. My life back on "planet normalcy" was a good life, and it was far easier than the one I have now. Yet, when I watch my sweet little whirlwind running in the sunshine, flapping his arms and giggling at some joke only he understands, I feel more blessed than I could have ever imagined. You could have had my son, but you didn't. He is mine, and I'm keeping him—probably for the rest of my life.

3

TYPICAL PARENTING SKILLS ARE NOT ENOUGH

e may become parents on the day our first child is born, but our parenting skills take longer to develop. They start as a bunch of ideas we've gathered from our environment: our parents, our relatives, our friends, and the media. We might have picked over those ideas and discarded outdated or harmful ones or those we're certain are for folks not as enlightened as ourselves, but for the most part we didn't invent these ideas. We absorbed them.

When we got pregnant, our ideas about child-rearing began turning into plans. We came to conclusions and etched those plans into stone. We became sure that we knew *the proper way* to raise children, and we decided to do so accordingly. We

would never spank. Our children would watch only 1 hour of television a day. Our marriage would always be a priority. Bribing and manipulating children is bad, so instead, we would help them develop their ability to reason and make good choices.

Then our children are born, and we try to put our plans into action. This is where things get really exciting. We discover that keeping a toddler clean is like having to tidy up the Augean stables. Hercules could do it, but he had help from the gods. We find that breakables left where children can reach them tend to get broken, even though we decided long ago that children need to be respectful of other people's belongings. Our cars begin to smell like old French fries and sour milk, and the dog now lives under the table, where the kids can't reach him. We come to the conclusion that we're lousy parents. In desperation, we turn to the highest authority we have available to us. We call Mom.

Mom laughs. She's been waiting for this phone call for years. She laughs *a lot*. She makes you hang on for a moment so she can repeat what you said to Dad. He laughs, too. Then Mom tells you how darling your children are and that they must be advanced, because they learned how to write four-letter words on your wall in ketchup far sooner than your cousin's children did. Then you get to listen to several stories about what a rotten little brat you were—stories that your aunts can corroborate because the tales about what you did have become family legend.

Finally, Mom settles down to business. She sets you straight. She tells you everything she's learned about raising children, and, if she's really nice, she does it without reminding you of your sanctimonious preaching of just a few short months ago. She tells you about natural consequences, like when a kid eats the cat's dinner, he shouldn't get dessert, and he must fill the dish back up so the cat won't starve. She tells you that leashes for kids are good safety tools, especially for teenagers. She also reassures you that 20 minutes of playing in toilet water won't kill your toddler, although the things he flushed away are gone for good.

Mom saves the day, or at least part of it. I mean, she's your mother—are you going to believe *everything* she says? So you ask your friends who have kids, and you ask your pediatrician, and you read some magazines to find tried-and-true parenting solutions. Slowly but surely, you build up your toolbox of tricks, and everything pretty much works out okay.

That is the ancient and time-honored way of learning parenting skills. But, sometimes it doesn't work.

If you have a child with special needs, you're pretty much on your own. Unless your mother raised a child with autism, she probably doesn't know what to do for a child who refuses to be held and cries every time you touch him. Or how to teach a nonverbal 5-year-old how to speak. Or how to get a 7-year-old to quit pulling chunks of hair out of his head so he can throw them into the air and watch them fall. Chances are, your mother's advice is going to be useless at best, if not downright disastrous.

And your friends? Unless they've got a child with special needs, they won't even understand your questions. "What do you mean, your child doesn't know how to make friends?" Parenting books and magazines are useless, too. They only tell you that your child is probably just fine, and if you're really worried, you should talk to his doctor. They don't tell you what to do if something's actually wrong. They gloss over that and move on to how to throw the perfect birthday party. Your pediatrician is great for diagnosing and prescribing medicine to treat some of the symptoms of autism but is typically not much help for behavioral problems, like when your child acts like a dog on the playground, complete with sniffing the backsides of other children.

Where do parents go next? To the Internet? It's a wonderful tool, capable of generating a vast amount of information. It does so in seconds and dumps out a great big pile. There's gold in that pile—you just have to be able to sort it from the hooey. Unfortunately, if you knew how to recognize the good from the bad in the first place, you probably wouldn't have had to search the Internet at all. Support groups are wonderful and nurturing, as long as the members are actively seeking answers instead of just sitting around complaining. Specialists and therapists who know about your child's disabilities are fantastic, if you can find them in your area and can pay their fees.

It's not easy being the parent of a child with special needs. Trying to use the parenting skills most of us arrive with is like trying to fix a computer with a buzz saw and a spatula. They're great tools—they're just not the ones we need.

Please understand that we've tried all the skills we have to help our children and ourselves. We're doing the best we can with what we know how to do. It's not enough. We need to find someone who knows about the challenges our kids face and can teach us something new. We need more than the typical set of parenting skills, and we need them now.

4

I HAVE NO ONE TO GUIDE ME

Most pediatricians are not trained to treat children with autism. Some know how to recognize autism and will provide a diagnosis, but few of them do more than tell parents that the school will take care of their child's difficulties. It's rare to find a doctor who knows what our kids need, what the local schools will and won't do, and what to tell parents to watch for. Parents walk into the office with concerns and typically walk out with those same concerns. At best, they get a word or a phrase written on a piece of paper—a diagnosis that other professionals will often dispute. Rarely do they depart with any idea of what to do next.

Pediatricians are not evil or stupid. Autism disorders are new to their world, and doctors are still

catching up, especially when it comes to treating children with mild autism. They're learning, but they're not there yet. Certainly they're not to the point where they can offer parents an education on autism or an outline of the child's current difficulties or of difficulties yet to come.

If a parent brings a child in and says he has terrible anxiety and is threatening to hurt himself, a doctor will refer the child to the necessary mental health specialist. But few doctors yet know that most kids with autism experience anxiety and anger issues and would benefit from learning emotional control before they get to the point of self-destruction.

Few pediatricians keep tabs on the occupational-therapy programs schools offer to see if they're sufficient or need to be supplemented elsewhere. They don't refer children for more in-depth testing, such as that used for visual tracking or auditory processing disorders. They don't give parents a list of assessments that need to be done, either by school personnel or by other medical and mental health professionals. They don't know what questions to ask parents to keep tabs on their patients' development. Typically, they tend to ignore the autism unless things get drastic. In the meantime, they refer parents to the local public school.

But the schools often aren't good resources for getting guidance, either. It worries me that the law limits what you can and can't tell me and that you hold the purse strings that pay for my child's therapies and education. This means that whenever you give me advice, there is always a question in the back of my mind about whether or not what you're advising is in my child's best interest—or your own. Are you telling me he doesn't need an aide because you feel he's ready to work on the next step toward learning independence? Or is it because you just don't want to pay the aide's salary? Because of the way the educational system is set up, there's a good chance I may not feel comfortable relying on your judgment. So, while your advice is helpful, it may not provide me with the guidance I feel I need.

As a parent, my child's pediatrician and school are my primary resources. Right now, there really is no other place I can go to get help in overseeing my child's overall development. I may be fortunate enough to hook up with specialists—a psychiatrist, neurologist, gastroenterologist, orthopedist, dietician, or a therapist or two. These professionals are godsends to our family. Their advice and hard work help my child immensely, but these specialists work independently of one another. I am the one who has to evaluate their opinions, coordinate the treatments, communicate their wishes to the school, and look to the overall development of my child.

When a need appears, I'm the one that has to determine its cause and decide the best place to get help. Is this problem due to my child's sensory issues? Is talking with the school's occupational therapist my best choice? Or is this issue part of normal childhood development? Is my child's behavior a reaction to his medication? How can I relay his teacher's observations to his psychiatrist? She tells me things and I take them to the doctor, then he asks me questions I can't answer. I can go back to the teacher, but the psychiatrist is busy and it will be weeks before we can get another appointment.

I have a hard enough time finding answers to the problems we face today, let alone trying to guess what difficulties my child may have in the future. What do we need to do *now* to prepare him for later? Do we wait until he's in high school and struggling to keep up with taking notes in class, and then regret not giving him more occupational therapy when he was in elementary school? Who's going to tell me what we need to do today? It's not enough that we're getting him through school this week or this year. What does he need to be as competent and happy an adult as possible? Who do I talk to about that?

Right now, there is no place I can go to get overall treatment advice about my child. I need one. I need a reliable autism center or a doctor who specializes in autism. I need someone who knows more about autism than I do to oversee his development and help me coordinate his therapies. I need help, and I need it now.

5

HOOEY

I'm being bombarded by information about autism. Unfortunately, 80% of it is false, misleading, or downright dangerous.

Up until a few years ago, it was hard to find information about autism and almost impossible to find any about mild autism. Now it seems to be on the cover of every magazine and newspaper—from *Newsweek* to *Glamour* to *Parenting*. My library and local bookstores have dozens of books, few of which agree with one another. Celebrities appear on my television, telling me how to cure my child. Some doctors are telling me autism is incurable, but others say they've found the answer. Google lists more than 18 million Web sites about autism, and most of them are selling something.

While some of the information is valid and helpful, most of it is hooey. The hooey may be the product of well-meaning, misinformed people, but there's a good chance it's been produced by someone in search of profit. For every tear we shed, someone tries to make a buck off of us. It's an ugly aspect of human nature and is unfortunately nothing new.

During my search for answers, I've been told so many things that sometimes I have a hard time sorting fact from fiction. I've heard that almost all doctors are pawns of the pharmaceutical companies, except for a few special ones, the only ones who really care about our kids. But they don't take insurance (insurance doesn't take them), and they happen to be very, very expensive. I've heard of special laboratories that run tests other labs can't because no one else knows how to do them. (If your child's results come back positive it means he needs the treatment; if they come back negative it means his body is retaining the toxins and he *really* needs the treatment.)

I've heard that my son's autism is my fault because I didn't play with him enough when he was a baby. I read that in many cases, autism is caused by using hair dye during pregnancy or having breast implants (but sources of information like these are anonymous). I've heard that one side of my son's brain grew more quickly than the other—thank goodness, though, there's a doctor who knows how to cure that. I've heard that vaccines cause autism—some researchers proved it, but other researchers say the first ones were wrong, and then there's another set of researchers who say the second batch of researchers was either paid off or they don't know what they're talking about.

I've heard that antidepressants can help, but if you pick the wrong one your child may commit suicide. I've heard of natural, behavioral, pharmaceutical, and psychiatric treatments, occupational therapy, sound therapy, deep nerve stimulation, spinning and bouncing therapy, magnesium supplements, Applied Behavioral Analysis, Floortime, TEACCH (Treatment and Education of Autistic and Related Communication-Handicapped Children), Relationship Development Intervention, staring deeply into a child's eyes until he is cured, having him wear colored lenses, enforcing sensory diets, reading social stories, offering special diets, taking dietary supplements, employing rubber chickens (for social-skills therapy), injecting vitamins, doing chelation therapy (stripping the body of heavy metals), taking hyperbolic oxygen treatments, having more parental consistency, using physical punishment, using restraint, putting children into isolation rooms or quiet rooms, giving more parental attention, making my son use his words instead of just giving him what he wants, taking the advice of Super Nanny, and getting a dog.

It's a lot of information. Some of it is great and would really help my kid. Some of it would waste my time and money and may even harm my child. But I can't always tell which is which. A lot of people are telling me that their solution is the right one, and some of them insist that if I don't listen to them, I'm a horrible parent who doesn't love my child. What if later I find out I could have cured him but I didn't try, because I didn't want to spend the money or because the treatment was too inconvenient for me? What if my choice hurts him? What if it kills him?

Even if I try to dig deeper for information, I may have difficulties. Chances are, I'm not a research scientist. I have no training in reading a study and evaluating it properly. Is a particular study well done? Is its population selected in an unbiased manner? Are its data statistically significant? Are the statistics it presents relevant or misleading? Who funded the study and why? Were the tests they used valid? How do they relate to tests used by other researchers? Are the study results repeatable? How is the study received by other researchers in the field? Why? Are the tests they used really measuring what they set out to measure? Were the data collected in a trustworthy manner? Major peer-reviewed medical journals sometimes can't sort this stuff out; they think a study is good science and publish it, only to retract it later. If they sometimes have trouble evaluating studies, how am I going to do it?

Sometimes I may disagree with you. It's not because I'm delusional, stupid, or lazy. Sometimes I'm doing the best I can just to swim in the flood of information directed toward parents of autistic children. If you think you have an answer for me, by all means share it. But don't be offended if I keep searching for another. After all, you may not be a research scientist, either.

6

SOCIAL REJECTION

When your child has autism, taking him on a trip to the grocery store is like running the gauntlet. If you're physically able to pick up your child, you put him in the shopping cart, even if he's too big. Failing that, you keep your eyes and perhaps a hand on him at all times. Otherwise he may run—into the parking lot or the wine section or the aisle of cleaning products. As you make your way through the store, you stay in the middle of the aisle to reduce his ability to grab things from the shelf. You make sure he has his comfort objects with him or something on hand to distract him. You do everything you can think of to increase the odds of making it through the store with as little trouble as possible.

You can't control everything, though. He can still see things he really, really, really has to have right now, or his world will fall apart in a big way. Buzzing fans, flickering lights, or cold refrigerated sections may overwhelm him and send him into a tantrum. Watching another shopper taste-test the grapes may trigger loud, indignant demands for punishment of the thief. Or, your child may decide to do something really unusual that makes sense to him and no one else, like licking the person in front of you in the checkout line.

Your child has perfectly good reasons for his behaviors. Unfortunately, they are not obvious to the people around you. Folks with autism don't have a giant "A" tattooed on their foreheads. They look like everyone else. When you're out in public and your child acts in a socially inappropriate manner, you're lucky if bystanders just think your child is strange. Typically, however, they assume he's an obnoxious brat whose idiot parents don't discipline him properly. Unless the child is 16 years old and 6 feet tall, in which case they may think he is dangerous.

You can almost always tell what the people around you are thinking, because they give you looks of puzzlement and disapproval. They gather their children and walk away from you with expressions of shock and pity. Sometimes they stop to offer you some advice, too.

"If you'd just discipline him more, he wouldn't do those things."

"You're not *really* going to buy him that after the way he acted, are you?"

"Can't you keep your child under control?"

"What's wrong with your child?"

"Why is he doing that?"

"A good swat on the rear would take care of that."

"Is he retarded?"

"Your child is bad."

"If you were more firm at home, you wouldn't have this problem."

"We like you very much, but we'd rather you didn't bring your child."

And that's just from the adults. The things kids say are worse.

Now multiply these reactions by however many years your child has been mobile and all the places you've visited together—not just the grocery store but every public place you've ever taken your child. The park. The library. The movies. Doctors' offices. Your parents' house. Sunday school and church. Other kids' birthday parties. Family reunions. His classroom. Are you beginning to get the picture?

Imagine watching your child run over to play with other children on the playground, only to have the group disband as he nears. Then the kids regroup somewhere else, and when he tries to join them, they run away again. Picture your teenager sitting alone in the school lunchroom while kids talk under their breath as they pass by him. "Freak." "Weirdo." Imagine your grown child never having a friend or a romantic relationship because he's unable to grasp the nuances of social interaction.

Years of rejection can make someone a little touchy and a tad defensive. It's human nature. If you watch your child get rejected enough times, you lose your trust in people. It's easier to withdraw than to take a chance again. You start to see disapproval in people's eyes even if it isn't there, because you know it's just a matter of time until it appears.

So, yes, I might be oversensitive when it comes to my child, and he might be touchy, too. We may both be defensive and quick to react at times. We may retreat behind walls of silence, blame, or denial. It's a double-edged self-defense mechanism that's enabled us to face each new day, even if it has caused our feelings of exclusion to grow.

The choices you make now when you interact with my child mean more to us than you know. Your opinion and your reactions are amplified in our eyes. Will your interactions with him be another drop in the tide of rejection we've lived with his whole life? Or, instead, will they be a lifeboat—a small space of acceptance and stability, where he feels safe and he can learn to make his way toward the shore of social acceptance? It may take a while for us to trust you and even longer for us to trust society as a whole. But you can't imagine how much we'd like to try.

7

GIVING ME ADVICE

I f you tell someone that your child has autism, there's a good chance they'll give you advice. Depending on how much they think they know about the subject, it may be a little, or it may be a lot. A whole lot. They don't have to know you well or know your child at all—they've got answers, and they want to share them.

The advice is kindly meant. They want to help me and my child, and bless them for that. But sometimes the advice just adds to my confusion, and sometimes it's downright insulting. Some of it assumes that simple parenting skills, which I apparently lack, will fix my child. And heaven forbid I don't actually follow the advice people give me. They've handed me the solutions that will help my child, and

I'm ignoring them. What kind of terrible parent does that make me?

When my son was little and not talking, I was told many times, "If you would just make him ask for things when he wants them, he'll start to talk." Well, I was already doing that and it wasn't working. Human communication is a lot more complicated than just expressing wants, even for a 3-year-old. School districts must agree with me, or they wouldn't be spending all that money on giving kids speech therapy.

Apparently, spanking your child is also very effective for curing autistic traits. I'm not sure how spanking affects brain development, exactly, but from the suggestions I've collected at the grocery store, I've learned that "knocking some sense" into kids not only takes care of autism, but it puts an end to all kinds of behavioral difficulties—even those caused by other neurological conditions. Or so I'm told.

Once I was informed by a doctor that it was obvious my child was depressed because he wasn't making eye contact. But, for only $5000 worth of treatment (which was not covered by insurance), this doctor could cure my son's depression and his autism, too.

Parents of other kids with autism tell me that my child can be cured. They've got lists upon lists of therapies I simply must do, no matter what they cost or how little evidence exists to prove they work. If my son still has autism, I'm to blame, because it means I don't care enough about him to do what it takes to give him a happy life.

A lot of people have told me that the schools can fix my child, but they don't want to because it's too expensive, and teachers don't like kids much anyway. But, they say if I hire the right lawyer or advocate, they can make it happen. There's just no way my child will get into quality programs unless I file due process against the school, even if I like his teachers and even if my son is showing good results with the programs they provide.

My child's doctor said he should take medicine, but people on the Internet say it will hurt him, so instead I should give him copper, magnesium, supplements, Epsom salt baths, and this really great stuff that you get at the health food store. It comes in a purple bottle and the lady behind the counter says it really works great and is completely safe, no matter what other medicines my child is taking or what his diagnosis is. *I don't think so.*

I've been told my kid belongs in special-education classes. I've also been told he should *never* ever be in special-education classes. I've heard it's okay to start him there and work toward including him in regular classes, but you have to watch the school really carefully to make sure they don't just leave him in special education and forget about him. Some people tell me the schools never want to include our kids in regular classes because it costs too much to pay for aides and supports. Others say the schools want to shove all our kids in regular classes because it costs less. They also tell me that the school will lie about the best placement for my child and that the main goal of teachers is to kick out the children who aren't "good enough" for their school. The one thing everyone agrees on is that if I let the school put my son in the wrong class, then I'll damage him forever.

I've heard that instead of sending my child to school, I need to homeschool him, or else attending regular school will harm his psyche irreparably because that's what happened to the child of someone they heard about on the Internet. On the other hand, everyone knows that if my son doesn't go to school with other kids, he won't learn how to get along with his peers and he'll be weird all his life.

People have told me that to help my child I have to take away the things he loves best—that I should never let him play with his trains again, even though he really, really likes them. But a doctor once told me

I have to make him take his trains wherever he goes so he'll build up an aversion to trains and never want to be around them again and that this will cure his obsessive nature. They all agree that the sooner we make him give up one of the few things that makes him happy, the happier he will be.

My son is in special-education PE, but I've been told that since he can catch a ball, he doesn't need it anymore and that I absolutely have to move him to regular PE. But someone else told me that in regular PE he'll be exposed to a lot of bullies, especially in the locker room, and by the way did you hear what happened to that kid three states over when his mom put him in regular PE? Another someone asked me how my kid is going to learn to deal with the jerks if we always protect him from bullies? And also, don't bother reporting bullying incidents to the school because they don't care if your kid gets hurt.

Let's not forget that wonderful professional who once explained to me that I had caused my child's autism because I didn't play with him enough when he was a baby. She firmly believed the "refrigerator mother" theory, even though it was disproved more than 30 years ago. Her advice was that it was too late now to fix my child. I should keep working on it, of course, but I shouldn't get my hopes up.

Over the years, I've gotten a lot of advice. Each person who's offered it has given it out of the kindness of their heart, because they wanted to help me and my child. Each person knew they had found the answer to our problems, and if only I followed their guidance, my child's life would be better. Most days I can thank them for their compassion, even if from where I stand, their advice is useless to me. But some days I can't. Some days I'm lost in the forest of demands, emotions, exhaustion, information, and decisions that autism brings, and my politeness slips. It's not okay that I'm rude, but sometimes I am.

It's fine that you offer me advice. Getting advice is an important way we gather information so we can help our children. Sifting through that advice to pull out the nuggets of wisdom is part of my job as a parent. I may use your ideas, or I may not. Or I may tuck them into my pocket, and someday when I'm really at my wits' end, I'll remember them. So please don't push me. I may not take your advice today, but I may use it tomorrow.

8

MY GOALS FOR MY CHILD

Before I knew my child had difficulties, my goals for him were simple: to enjoy life, love, and happiness—the same plan all parents have for their children. Having wealth, independence, and a few grandchildren were in there somewhere too, because that's just the way parents are. We want our children to be able to leave the nest someday and have the skills needed to go build one of their own.

When things started to get tough, my goals changed. For a while, it was enough just to have my son live to reach adulthood. In those days of his whirlwind activity and little common sense, I was sure I'd lose him. *Just let him live,* I prayed. *Whatever comes next I will deal with, but don't let me lose him*

before he's 3 years old. When he made it to the age of 3, I prayed he would make it to 5 years. And when he made it that far, I prayed he would make it to 7.

Slowly, as he grew, his life became more stable. I realized there was a very good chance he would make it to adulthood. Then what? How would my son live as an adult? Would he be dependent on me? Or (an even scarier thought) dependent on someone else? Would he be naive and unsuited for facing the challenges of the real world? Would he land himself in prison? After all, social blunders that are no-no's when you're 6 years old become criminal offenses by the time you're 20. More than anything else, I wanted to enjoy the relative safety of normalcy. If my son was "normal," then he would be ready at some point to face the world on his own. I wanted someone, somewhere, to find a way for my little boy to grow up to be just like all the other kids. I didn't want him to have a hard life, and I didn't want one for myself either. I wanted *normal*.

It took a few more years for me to figure out that "normal" wasn't going to happen. My boy wasn't going to be a typical kid. Not now, not ever. He would improve and build skills and mature, but his autism was always going to be there, waiting and setting traps here and there for the rest of his life. It was a hard realization for me. My goals evaporated. As I came to understand that there was no path to reach them, I let them go. Instead, I kept my eyes on today and what was immediately in front of us, ignoring a future I didn't want to contemplate. If he could be 10 years old forever, tucked here under my wing, I thought maybe then I could keep him safe, and perhaps I could make sure he had a happy life. I replaced my goals with denial to preserve my sanity.

I hadn't given up; not really. I was taking a breather. I indulged in an emotional trip past reality so I could heal myself enough to face tomorrow, enough to look down deep and find my sweet little boy again in that jumble of blue jeans and dirty sneakers and differences. He wasn't going to be a typical kid, not now, not ever, but that was okay. He was still wonderful, even with one foot in another world. His life would be filled with challenges, but that's what life is; with or without autism, everyone has hills to climb. He had skills and talents—we could build on them. His weaknesses wouldn't be so bad if he was aware of them and had tools to work around them. His life might be difficult, but that was okay, because I could help him find his place in the world.

So what do I want for him now? Life, love, and happiness—the same hopes all parents have for their children. Wealth, independence, and a few grand-children are in there, too, but if those things aren't in the cards for us, it's okay. Happiness and security will be enough for me.

9

MY CHILD'S DEVELOPMENTAL PATH

Many people with mild autism contributed to building our country's space program. Men and women who were fascinated with computers, engineering, and the stars focused their attention on the millions of details that make up a spacecraft and its support systems. Together, they helped build a pathway for space exploration and gathering knowledge about what exists beyond our planet.

Chefs have a fair number of people with mild autism in their ranks. Their extra-sensitive palates, their relentless passion to refine their results, and their insistence on maintaining structure and routines in their kitchens to ensure cleanliness and safety are necessary attributes in a chef. They're all traits of autism, too.

More than a few musicians and composers are on the autism spectrum. They play until their fingers bleed, and their extra-sensitive hearing and unique memories allow them to be able to turn the sounds in their minds into music that captivates us. Mathematicians, statisticians, and accountants are fascinated by numbers. They focus on details, enjoy routine, and are able to see the patterns mathematics make. Lawyers have encyclopedic memories and a relentless drive. Surgeons have an excellent grasp of spatial relationships, vast stores of knowledge, and a fascination with making complex body systems work as they should. While not all people who practice these trades have autism, many do.

It is believed that Nikola Tesla, Albert Einstein, and Thomas Edison may have had mild autism. Generations of lesser-known men and women have also used their autistic attributes to lead happy and productive lives. Their ability to hyperfocus and their attention to detail were called "persistence" and "craftsmanship." Their fascination with special interests led them to become experts in their fields. They found trades that capitalized on their overresponsive sensory systems, and they improved their social skills until they no longer served as a barrier to finding employment or having relationships. Many people have succeeded in life not only despite their autism, but in some ways, because of it.

As a parent, I know this. I've seen examples of successful people in the books and articles I've read about autism, in the lectures I've attended, and in my consultations with experts. I've heard the stories from other moms in our group; we pass them around like soldiers passing a bottle of spirits around a campfire. They give us hope and courage and keep us warm and able to face tomorrow. These folks made it; our kids can, too. We tell this to each other and to ourselves, and we believe it. Most days.

But, we've all heard stories about the other people, too—the ones who are unable to overcome the difficulties autism can bring. We've heard about the lonely men and women, who are at odds with their families and who long for an intimate relationship but can't maintain one. There are people who are tormented by obsessive-compulsive disorder or who are so socially naive, they are in danger of being preyed upon. Unhealthy, inappropriate, or "odd" behaviors have kept a number of people from working or living independently. Some who lack an understanding of social concepts and have an inability to control their anger wind up in jail. And sadly, there are anxiety-driven adults and children who finally decide that suicide offers them the peace they couldn't find in life.

We've heard these stories, too. We don't talk about them, but we think about them.

The scary part is that there aren't any predictors that can tell us how our children will turn out. There are many people who were severely affected by autism as children, but thanks to therapeutic interventions, improved communication skills, medications, and a large dose of determination and passion, they have grown into fully functioning adults. They still have autism, but they cope with life well. There are also people whose strengths and weaknesses change very little throughout their lives. And there are children who begin life well but are overtaken later by uncontrollable anxiety, rage, and other issues that follow them into painful and sometimes dangerous adulthoods.

As I watch my child grow, I see him follow each of these paths at different times. Sometimes he's doing great. Other days aren't so good. Some days are scary, and sometimes days can turn into weeks and months of "scary." We may be doing well now, but we've had the rug pulled out from under us before, many times. I know it could happen again, and there is no way I can stop it.

If I knew that my son had a good chance of ultimately being able to lead a happy adult life, I could live with the scary times. I could stay productive and positive and deal with today, so we can reach tomorrow. But I don't know this for certain. Neither do his doctors, teachers, therapists, or any other expert out there. There is no set developmental path for our kids. There are no indicators for how children with specific types of autism will develop. Therapies and interventions are essential. Good parenting is crucial. A great environment is priceless. But too often, these things aren't enough. Despite all our efforts, some of our kids don't make it. I've met their parents and cried with them and wondered if, someday, their pain is going to be mine.

Some kids with autism do well in life, and some don't. What will happen to mine?

10

THE GRIEVING PROCESS

Sometimes, when I go to pick my child up after school and see him walking next to his typically developing classmates, I cry.

The other kids move like fish in a school, each traveling their own trajectory but with a sameness of movement that comes with typical development. Boys rush headlong or do the pre-puberty strut. Girls dart around in giggly groups. Adolescents saunter along as if they are establishing their territory with each step. They call out to one another and laugh, exchanging gossip and doing the social dance that dominates their world.

My son walks through the other kids as though they are bits of landscape. With his weight balanced forward on his toes and his rigid gait, he navigates

the crowd in a world of his own. Other people are obstacles to him—he pays enough attention to avoid collisions but doesn't look at their faces. Subtle social clues are lost on him; even overt gestures often go unnoticed. A child who waves at him doesn't register unless the kid speaks loudly enough to get his attention. Smiles of friendship, raised eyebrows, smirks of derision—they pass him by undigested and uninterpreted.

The kids from my son's class last year are among the crowd. I see how they've grown, matured, and taken steps toward joining the adult world of having relationships and responsibilities. Their clothing tastes have changed. The girls' skirts are shorter, the boys' pants baggier. I see makeup and whiskers. And boobs.

My son is wearing his favorite sweatshirt—the same one he's worn for years. It's zipped to his chin with the hood up, even though it's a warm day. The sweatshirt is blue, and it gives him comfort—it's a security blanket that helps my son keep himself contained. I love that he loves it. But I hate that he still needs it.

I am proud of my son, and I'm so very proud of all the things he's accomplished, even with his difficulties. He's grown and matured and is on the path to adulthood, with whatever that may bring. He is different, and I've accepted that. I love him for who he is and no longer miss the boy he might have been. Yet some days, I still cry.

As the parent of a child with autism, my emotions have run the gamut. I've felt pride, elation, contentment, confidence, fear, anger, grief, self-pity, and despair. And I've felt love—there is always love. I wander through these feelings as I make my journey through his childhood and my parenthood. I, too, have matured along the way. I have come to accept many things, even though I have not always embraced them. But that doesn't mean that when circumstances change, I won't fall back into my emotional turmoil again.

My son is changing schools. What will happen? He wants to go to the dance. Did you see the way those girls looked at him and laughed? It wasn't nice. The school says he's ready to try attending math class without an aide. Can he make it without one? I'm getting older. Will I be here for as long as he needs me? He wants to have a birthday party. Who will come? Those kids are kind to him, but it doesn't mean they're his friends. My son's have-to-wear-on-Thursdays t-shirt is too small now, but they don't make it in his size now that he's bigger. He's not going to like having to change shirts. Graduation is coming up. What happens after that?

People talk about a grief process that one goes through when something traumatic happens, like when our children receive diagnoses and we find out they have special needs. They expect that, given time, we'll come to terms with our child's difficulties and accept them or "get over it." Dr Ken Moses has a different theory—that we wander around on a "grief map," traveling through different emotional states as events trigger them. I think he's almost got it right. His map concept fits perfectly, but labeling it a "grief map" implies that sadness is the overwhelming emotion our children create in us and that our actions are a product of that sadness. It doesn't account for the pride we have in our children, the love we feel, and the rest of the positive emotions that accompany us along our lifelong journey together. A "grief map" is just part of the story of why I do what I do.

Today, I shed a few tears. Tonight, when I see my son laugh hysterically at a movie he's watched 50 times before, it will make me smile. Tomorrow, who knows? I am calmer now than I was when we received his diagnosis, but my emotions are still my daily companions, now and forever.

11

HOPE AND DELUSIONS

Please be gentle with my delusions. I need them. They're intertwined with my hope, my confidence, and my motivation. Without them, I wouldn't be able to face my child's difficulties at all. My fears would overwhelm me, and so would my pain. I need to know that soon things will be all right—that if I just keep putting one foot in front of the other, someday my child's life will be easier, and so will mine. Someday the phone calls from school will stop, my child's friendships and coping skills will start, and I won't have to fear what happens when he has to live without me.

These particular delusions are healthy. They help me, and they help my child. Unfortunately, some of my delusions don't help anyone. Instead of

keeping me focused on the here and now, the today and tomorrow, they block my vision completely. When it comes to our children, we all wear tinted glasses. They're crafted from our love, pride, and fear. They were formed the day we discovered we were pregnant and continue to be forged throughout our children's lives. I wear the same glasses you do, but mine are also glazed with grief, guilt, pain, and anger. I desperately need to see my child clearly because my choices are so crucial, but right now I'm not able to. By blocking out his problems, I can also block out some of my own pain.

It's not okay if I don't believe you or if I ignore what you say when you tell me something I don't want to hear. But if I convince myself that you're wrong, then I don't have to face the fact that my child's difficulties are that bad.

It's not okay if I expect you to "fix" my child or tell you that if he still has difficulties, it must be because you don't know what you're doing or because you don't care. But I want so desperately to believe that my child is fixable.

It's not okay for me to insist that my child be placed in a classroom that doesn't focus on his needs. It doesn't help him if I demand that he be mainstreamed even if he's not ready yet, because I believe that somehow the "normalcy" of the other kids will rub off on him. But, I'm not able to see today that he will be okay despite his differences. Right now, I just want his differences to go away.

It's not okay if I believe that it's your fault, because that way I'll know it's not mine.

It's not okay if I can't look at my child realistically. This is not fair to him or me or you. By doing so, I'm slowing his progress and causing us all frustration, anger, and anxiety. But, it's all I'm capable of right now. I'm simply not ready to accept everything at once. You can give me all the facts you want, but until I'm ready, they'll just spill over me, to be pushed aside or tripped over until I am able to face them another day.

Today, I'm not ready. Perhaps tomorrow, I will be. I may not be ready to accept it all, but maybe I can digest a little bit more than I did yesterday. Perhaps next week I could accept a little more, and some more the week after that. I ask that you be gentle and patient. My progress may not be fast. You may never see the results of the seeds you're sowing today or see me fully ready to embrace my child for what he is. But bit by bit, fact by fact, I will eventually get there.

Don't give up on me. My child and I need you.

12

ACCEPTANCE AND REALISM

P lease don't ask me to accept my child's autism. I won't, and I can't.

I can accept his bubbling laughter, which erupts each time he sees his favorite cartoon, even though the characters are meant to entertain kids years younger than he is. I can accept his fascination with things no one else cares about, like golf balls and hubcaps and the dinnerware used on the Titanic, and the passion he devotes to learning about them. I can accept his fabulous memory, even though it fails him at school but stands ready to collect and retain the most obscure bits of trivia. I treasure the jokes that only he understands, and his insistence that I enjoy them, too. I can take him to the zoo to see the elephants

again and again and again, just because they make him smile. I can do that.

I can even accept that he won't eat most foods and that his dietary menu rarely includes more than 10 items at any given time. I can accept that every day at school, even if it's 90 degrees outside, he wears a hooded jacket zipped all the way up to his nose because it makes him feel more secure. My son can do algebra, yet he can't cross the street by himself with any degree of safety. In school, instead of spending lunchtime chatting with his friends, he spends it in a corner of the library with his face buried in a book about the history of video games. If he ever learns to drive, it may be many, many years later than his classmates do. He may not develop the street smarts to make public transportation work for him, either. His personality may always make it difficult for him to keep a job, no matter how much his skills improve. I can accept all of these things, too.

What I can't accept is how the boys in PE class set him up to get in trouble, and how easily he falls for it, every time. Or the way the nice girls chat with him for a moment then move away, which is still better than the giggles and sarcasm the mean girls dish out. I can't accept that 40 birthday party invitations go out, but *not one child* comes to his birthday party.

Or that his unpredictable temper, which lands him in the principal's office now, may land him in jail in a few years, or, God forbid, the morgue. So far, we've been able to keep at bay the depression that comes from him realizing he is so different from the other kids, but one day that sadness may very well take him from me like it has taken so many other teens with autism. Someday, I will die and leave him alone to fend for himself in a world he does not understand. That I can't accept.

Don't ask me to accept his autism or come to terms with all the pain he will face in this lifetime because of it. I can't, and I won't. I can treasure him and love him and accept his quirks, but I can't welcome his difficulties. If I do, I've given us over to them, killed my hopes, and ended all our hard work. I will have decided that that's the way life will be—that all my fears can come true and that I'm okay with it. I'm not.

Instead of asking me to accept his autism, ask me to look carefully at how individual difficulties affect him today. That I may be able to do. I might be able to be realistic about today. But, if you want me to be able to listen to and accept what you're saying, you'll have to do more than just point out his problems. You'll need to suggest a path that may help him overcome his challenges—to defeat them or learn to work around them or at least be able to live with them. Show me the possibility of a better future for my child and the steps we can take to get there.

I can accept challenges, differences, hard work, and setbacks. What I can't accept is giving up and leaving my son's future to fate. Help me see my child's difficulties as obstacles to overcome, instead of unclimbable mountains. Then I can view autism as a journey and not the end of the road.

I may even learn to accept it.

13

MY OPTIONS

A fter I have done all I can do to help my child, he has only three other sources of treatment:

- What his doctor will do.
- What I can pay someone else to do.
- What his school will do.

That's it. If my child's life is to improve, those are our options. There is no magic wand on the list or a fairy godmother or a genie in a bottle who can make my child's autism go away. Our resources are our doctor, our outside resources, and our school.

My child's doctor is wonderful, but he has his limitations. His knowledge of autism is sketchy at

best, and medication can only do so much. It can calm my son's nerves and help him sleep; it can assist with his depression, focus his attention, and help him keep his anger under control. But it can't make him talk. It can't make him aware of the social world around him or push him into it. It won't teach him the thousands of things he'll need to know to be a functioning, successful adult. All it can do is set the stage. It can't help him perform.

If I'm lucky, I may live near therapists who know about autism, though in most places they are pretty scarce. I might have to drive a little, an hour or two, three to five times a week, but it's worth it to find someone who understands children with autism and provides the kinds of therapies they need: behavioral training, speech and language therapies, social skills training, emotion management classes, occupational therapy, and more. Professionals who offer therapies like these can change lives. They can't cure my child's autism, but they can help him an awful lot. However, all their knowledge and dedication comes at a price. A big one. One my insurance often won't pay, even though the therapies have been scientifically proven to work. My child would benefit from receiving these therapies; they could change his life and mine. But right now, most insurance companies don't pay for the autism treatments our children need.

In many cases, state agencies have stepped up to the plate. They've determined that some children's difficulties are severe enough that the state will foot the bill for the enormous fees the therapy clinics charge. They'll spend the hundreds of thousands of dollars it takes to get the therapies that make such a difference in the lives of these kids and their families. Bless the state for doing what it can to help our children. And bless the families; their road is hard, and they need all the help they can get. But kids at the mild end of the autism spectrum need help, too. The state doesn't always see it that way, and these children are often left with no services at all. Therapy could help them, but the children can't get therapy unless their parents have the money it takes to pay for it. Most don't.

So, my child's school may be my only hope. If he is going to receive the therapies he needs, it must come from you. I don't know how you're going to pay for it. I don't know how you're going to find and retain specialists to perform the therapies. I don't know how you're going to fit 50 hours of academic and therapeutic instruction into a 30-hour school week, or how you're going to convince your general-education teachers that now they're going to teach special-education children too, or how you're going to get the other kids on the playground to accept my child, or how you're going to meet the individual needs of all your students. I don't care how you do it. I just want you to be the magic wand that can help my child.

It isn't fair for me to place all my hopes on you to help my child. But right now, there may be no place else for me to put them.

14

DEALING WITH TRANSITIONS

T ransitions are hard on my child. They're even harder on me.

They scare me to death because I haven't got a clue what situation we'll land in. This year's teacher may have been wonderful—full of compassion, trained to teach kids with autism, innovative, patient, persistent—a teacher with high standards for herself and for her students. She may have been a fabulous teacher for my son, but that doesn't mean next year's teacher will be even half as good.

We've had one or two teachers before who were a bad fit for my child, and so have most other parents I know. We've had teachers who didn't understand autism or our kids—who didn't know why people with autism do what they do. There

have been teachers who blamed our child's autism on our parenting skills, punished our kids for things that were beyond their control, and ignored or discarded our kids as being less important than other children. We've had teachers who just didn't know how to reach our children and propel them forward, so school turned into a babysitting session that wasted some of the few short years we have to teach our kids what they need to know to survive on their own.

Most of our teachers have been fabulous, and yet I know there are teachers out there who still don't understand my child and may not care to. The grade levels that lay behind us had a few, and the ones ahead will likely have one or two. Each year, when my child receives his classroom assignment, he runs the risk of being paired with a teacher who can create 9 months of misery for him and for me. His school administrator may be able to make sure he's assigned to a teacher who is a good fit, if she knows her teachers and if she knows my son. But, in these days of tenure, budget cuts, and overcrowded classrooms, she may not have as many options for placement as she'd like.

The teacher and administrator are only part of the equation, however. The other kids in my child's

class play a part, too. It only takes one mean classmate to make my son's life a torment, one child who
decides that his naïveté and intolerance make him
a perfect target or that his differences make him a
freak.

"Hey, I'm your friend. I forgot my lunch money—be a nice guy and give me yours."

"The teacher thinks it's really funny when people
make mooing sounds every time she talks."

"Touch me there. Teacher! Guess what he did!"

"Don't talk to him. He's weird."

"Get away from me, loser."

Or maybe everyone else will be great, but my
kid bottoms out. Maybe this will be the year he just
can't keep up anymore. His inability to control his
frustration could turn math class into a minefield,
setting him off at any time. His weak social understanding might make analyzing literature impossible.
The maturity required to navigate his new school
campus just might not have developed yet. We've
made it so far, but sometimes it has been by the skin
of our teeth. Who's to say we'll make it next year?

Transitions scare me. I don't know where we'll
land, and I don't know if we'll be up to the challenge. I don't know what you're going to do if things
aren't working.

Are you going to leave us in a bad situation? Will you tell me it's my child's fault or mine or "that's just the way things go" or "there's nothing we can do"? It's happened to us before. I don't want it to happen again, and I don't want things to change and I don't want to try anything new. And if we have to do this transition anyway, then I'm going to be nervous at best and horrible at worst.

But if I know you and trust you, if I know you like my child and are working to help him succeed, then maybe I'll be able to relax. If I know you're keeping an eye on my child and are ready to help, that you're not just leaving him to sink or swim, then maybe our transition will go smoother. If I'm aware going into it that most transitions are tough in the beginning but adjustments can be made, and that my child and his teachers can learn and adapt, then maybe I can calm down and do a better job of helping my child through the change. Tell me we'll meet 30 days after the transition to see how things are going and that if we need to make adjustments, we will. Let me know that you care about my child and that you'll work hard to put him in a situation where he can succeed.

Help me learn to trust you. Then maybe I can relax and help make this transition work.

15

CHILDHOOD DEVELOPMENT

I f I have a poor understanding of my child's strengths and weaknesses, it may not be because I'm in denial. It may be that I don't know a lot about what typical childhood development looks like.

Unless I've been around a lot of children, I probably won't know much about the typical stages of childhood development. I won't know what most kids are capable of at different ages or how they act. Without that information, I'll have nothing to use as a yardstick when it comes to evaluating my own child's behavior and abilities.

If I have no reference, I may not be a good judge of how smart he is. If he struggles with a homework assignment, is it because he has a problem, or is this a difficult concept for most kids his age? How do

the questions he asks and the things he says in class compare to the comments other kids make? Is his understanding on par with theirs, and is he ahead or behind? If he doesn't take tests well and his grades don't show a good picture of his intelligence, they give me no insights, either. It's possible that my view of his abilities may be very different than yours.

I also might not see how his organizational skills stack up against those of other kids his age. At home, he may do great on his chores because I've designed them to match his ability levels, but at school he'll be expected to have the same skills as his peers. At home, I may think it's okay that I have to remind him three times to brush his teeth, but at school, his classmates might reasonably be expected to turn in their homework with no reminder. If I don't understand his classmates' abilities, I may not understand or agree with your assessment of his.

My lack of knowledge probably extends to social development, as well. How many boys my son's age are a little slow to mature? How many think playing tag during sixth-grade recess is okay? In fourth grade, is it reasonable for him to ask his peers to play in the sandbox? Do kids his age swear? How about locker room talk? I know poor language at school is never acceptable, but what I need to know is whether his behavior is normal. Is my son becoming a pervert, or is his fascination with crude jokes just part of being an adolescent? At what point does it become worrisome?

What about his ability to deal with change, frustration, and anger? How much do I need to worry about his behaviors? Which ones do I need to worry about at all? Do most kids grow out of these? Which ones are too far out of the norm? Which ones are going to be far enough out that other kids will think he's weird? And how will I know how to evaluate the other kids' behavior toward my son?

If I don't understand the abilities of typically developing kids, I'll have a hard time evaluating the classroom placements you offer my child. I won't know the teacher's expectations, how fast the curriculum will move, how much help students will get, or how hard the work will be. I won't know how my child will fit in with the other students or understand how interactions with them may affect his social development. Without that knowledge, my perspective of the benefits and disadvantages of a particular classroom may be very different than yours.

If I can't judge my child's abilities against those of his peers, how can you and I agree on his strengths and weaknesses? Without having the same viewpoint, how do we come up with common goals? If I have little understanding about how your classroom works, how can we decide on an educational plan to meet those goals? You and I may be on different planets, looking for a meeting point. That's not likely to work. I might think you don't know what you're talking about, and you would probably think I'm in denial.

So how do we make it work?

Educate me. Let me into your classroom. I need to see how my child functions in relation to his peers. Let me watch him play on the playground or wander the campus. Let me see him at PE and at lunchtime, during math and language arts class. Let me observe him, as well as his classmates. Give me a chance to put his behavior into perspective. Then we can talk about his strengths and weaknesses and try to find some common ground.

If we don't come to an agreement about where my child is now, we can't decide how to get him to where we both want him to be. Help me see where you're coming from.

16

WHAT ARE
WE DOING?

As an educator, you have been working in the school system for years. You know how the special-education system works. You've had training and in-services to keep you up to date on new teaching methods and laws. If you need help, you've got a lot of coworkers who know the ropes. You've all worked together as teams before and gone through the IEP process many times. But this is my first time navigating the system, and sometimes I don't have a clue what's going on.

I don't know your vision. Are you putting my son into special education to help him, or will he fall through the cracks there and be left to fend for himself? Are you working to include students in general education as much and as soon as possible? Are you

just trying to push my child through the system, or are you preparing him to face the world? Unless you tell me, all I have to go on is what my mother said happened to my cousin 30 years ago.

I don't know your terms and your jargon. I don't know what an IEP or a 504 plan is. I don't know how they work, the differences between the two, which is a better fit for my child, or why I would want one over the other. I don't know what *No Child Left Behind, English Language Learners, Adequate Yearly Progress, accommodations, modifications, adapted PE, occupational therapy, assistive technology, behavioral intervention plan, dysgraphia, dyspraxia, executive function, fluency, Individuals with Disabilities Education Act, learning disabilities, language-based learning disabilities, Local Education Agencies, mainstreamed, fully included, Other Health Impairment, physical therapy, response to intervention, receptive language, specific learning disability, speech impaired, Special Education Local Plan Area,* or *research based* means.

I especially don't understand what you're talking about when you use the acronyms for any of these terms. You're speaking in a language I don't understand, and I haven't the faintest idea what you mean. But if I make the wrong choices, I know they could affect my child enormously, possibly for the rest of his life.

I don't know your assessments. The functional behavioral assessment, independent education evaluation, Connors test, norm-referenced test, Woodcock-Johnson tests, Kaufman test, Stanford-Binet Intelligence Scales, Wechsler Scales, Sequenced Inventory of Communication Development, Peabody Picture Vocabulary Test Revised, Targeted Brownsfields Assessments, Child Behavioral Checklist, Vineland Adaptive Behavioral Scales, and all the rest won't help me determine my child's strengths and weaknesses unless you help me understand what they are for—what they test, how they do it, what the results are, and what they mean. Unless I understand the assessments, I may not agree with your plans for his education.

I don't know your processes. I don't know that you're going to put a plan into place and then check up on my child in a few weeks to see how it's going. Or that, if things aren't going well, we can try something else. Or that if I'm not happy with my child's progress, I can call for another IEP meeting instead of having my child lose precious time by sitting in an inappropriate class. I don't know if you're planning on having a transition meeting for him in May. In

January, I start worrying about what the next school year will bring. By the end of March, I'm a nervous wreck, so I start pestering you about it, but by then I feel like if I hadn't said anything, then maybe the transition meeting wouldn't have happened at all.

I don't know why you're doing what you're doing. What is the overall set of skills you're trying to build in my son? Are you working on academic skills only? Or do you teach social and life skills, too? Are you wanting my child to spend part of his day in special-education classes without an aide, instead of spending all day in general-education classes with an aide, because you're trying to build his independence? I thought it was just because aides are too expensive. I don't know that you're peeling me off my kid a little bit more each year, because that's what you do with all parents so their kids become more independent. I thought you were kicking me out of the classroom or were reluctant to work with me.

I don't know who to talk to if there's a problem. I know I can talk to the teacher, but if I need more help, where do I go next? I can find my way to the principal, but I don't know that it's okay for me to go ask the resource teacher about how I can help my boy with homework or ask the speech teacher to clarify something for me. We have a director of special education? What does she do, and why? The rest of the administration is a complete mystery to me. But if I start asking the wrong people, I feel like I'm going to make someone mad, and someone will think I'm going over her head to talk to her boss. Then there will be trouble.

I don't even know who you all are. A whole host of you comes to my meetings, and I don't know who does what. There is a general-education teacher, a special-education teacher, a speech-language pathologist, an assistant principal, a counselor, a psychologist, an occupational therapist, an adapted PE teacher, a program specialist, a behavioral specialist, and a director of special education. All I see is a row of suits. You're all talking to each other in some kind of code, making decisions, and then wanting me to sign something that determines my child's fate. I'm really not following this.

Here's what I do know. I know what *Free Appropriate Public Education* is. It means you are required to give my child a good education. A mom in the parking lot told me all about it, and she had quite a bit to say. I know what an advocate is, because everyone on the Internet says I absolutely must have either a lawyer or an advocate or my child won't get the help he needs. I know you have classes I was never told about that might be really great for my kid. I found out about them from a parent in the support group I attend. He also told me about a private reading program that worked great for his child (because he said your program didn't), and since his kid is a lot like mine, he said I should sue you until you agree to pay for it. And don't even get me started about the things I learned on some of the hundreds of Web sites out there that can "train me to fight for my child." So even if you haven't educated me about your system, I've learned a lot on my own.

I am going to be a part of the team that decides the plan for my child's education. Please help me learn about your school system and how it works. Help me make sense of all the abbreviations and methods and job titles. Give me the information I need to make good decisions for my child. If you don't, I'll be forced to look for the information someplace else. One way or another, I'll find it.

17

YOUR CHALLENGES

I f the only things I know about your classroom are what I saw on "Back to School Night" and what my child tells me, I'm not going to know much about what your day looks like.

School was a lot different when I was a kid. From what I remember, kindergarten was about coloring pictures and listening to stories—not writing and being introduced to algebraic concepts. We had art class and music in every grade level, and we had PE every day. Now you've got to cram in so much instruction to meet higher standards that there's little time for electives. Things we were taught in seventh grade, you're now teaching in fifth or fourth grade. I didn't have much homework until junior high, and now kids are getting it in kindergarten

and even preschool. If I'm basing my expectations of your class on my childhood experiences, I'm likely to really underestimate the pace of your classroom.

I also don't have a clue about how much time you spend working after school. If I were to guess, I'd probably figure how long it takes you to grade my child's homework and multiply that by the number of kids in your class, then add in time for grading a few tests here and there. I don't see all the rest of the stuff you do—all the time you spend in curriculum meetings, preparing materials, doing research, sitting in training classes, serving on committees, leading extracurricular activities, and doing paperwork. All I see is what comes home.

Chances are, I don't know much about the other kids in your classroom, either. I may know a bit about some of them—Sarah is smart and Joe is really nice—but I probably won't know that Sophia is bipolar and Anthony can't read. I won't have a clue how many of your kids need extra help or don't speak our language well or have learning disabilities or don't bring back paperwork because their parents never complete it. I don't know about the kids who live with an addict or an abuser or have broken families or a parent in prison, and I won't have a clue about the foster kids in your class or those who are struggling with poverty or a chronic illness. If you're a general-education teacher, I'm likely to look at your classroom and see a bunch of typically developing kids and not remember that even typically developing kids have difficulties, too.

I don't know a lot about the laws and regulations you have to follow every day. I understand that confidentiality laws mean you can't tell other people about my child. But, it probably won't occur to me that they also mean that if we're discussing a problem my son is having with a classmate, you may not be able to tell me the whole story, because you have to protect that child's confidentiality, too. Or that a mom in the parking lot can say whatever she wants about how an outside program helped her kid so much more than your lousy one did, and you can't tell me if it really did or if her kid is just as far behind as he used to be. And you can't tell me why her son qualified for a bunch of services that my son isn't eligible for. It probably also doesn't dawn on me that the same laws that say you have to keep my sweet angel child in class while you teach him not to hit other kids means you can't boot out the rotten little snot who sits next to him and sometimes hits him first. And I may not have realized that you have to be careful how you help my child, because you can't discriminate against typically developing kids, either.

I don't know the challenges you face. You have demands on your time, skills, and patience that are unknown to me. Unless I'm part of the world of education, I just don't see them. But I need to know about them, if I'm helping to make decisions about my child's education. Without that information, it will be hard for me to tell the difference between what you can and can't do or what you just don't want to do.

Take the time to educate me. If I have an idea that's not feasible, don't assume it's because I'm too demanding or that I'm in denial. Instead, show me your world. Explain why you're doing what you're doing. Don't just say, "We move too fast for your child." Instead, show me the workload and let me help make the decision about whether my son can keep up. If you don't have time for a meeting today, let me know why—tell me you're off to a meeting or catching up from last week's training or tutoring other kids in the class who are struggling. Help me understand your position. That way, when it's time for us to sit down together and come up with a plan, I can help generate solutions that will work for both of us.

CAN I TRUST YOU?

18

I don't know you.

You are part of a large organization that I'm supposed to hand my child over to, and I don't know anything about you.

I've never met anyone from the district office. I don't know if the superintendent cares more about the bottom line than she does about kids with special needs or how much she really knows about our kids. Does she pay any attention to special education, or is it a department that gets swept under the rug? As long as no lawsuits are filed, how much effort really goes into the development of your special-education program?

What about the director of the special-education department? Is she a bureaucrat who knows nothing

about how a classroom really works? Is it her job to "handle" our complaints so we don't bother the rest of the district—you know, the "real" students, parents, and teachers? Does she know what it's like to stand in my shoes? Does she really care about my child learning the skills he needs, or does she just want to make sure the right boxes on our paperwork are checked so he gets pushed through the system on time?

I've met the principal a few times—in the hall-ways and in our meetings. She always smiles and says hello and seems friendly. But when I tell her I have a concern, I can see her face change just a little, and suddenly it feels like she becomes a politician. She starts choosing her words carefully, and her face takes on a practiced look, like she's trying to project an image of concern but she doesn't want her expression to give any information away. I can't tell what she's really thinking. I just know she's trying to calm me down without taking my concerns seriously. She keeps smiling though.

I know my child's teacher a little better. If I'm able to observe in the classroom, I probably know her fairly well—I've seen her in action. I know what is important to her and what is not, how she inter-acts with the kids, her expectations for classroom behavior, and how she treats my child and the rest of the class. I know if she likes my child. I know if she tries to help him. If she tells me something I don't want to hear, I can generally gauge whether she's complaining or informing me so I can help my child, or if she's blaming me for his behavior. And I know she's real. Inside that teacher is a real person, who's trying her best to rise to the challenges my child brings to her classroom. If I'm in her classroom, I can get to know her. I can watch her operate, and my trust grows.

But if I can't be in the classroom, then it's harder for me to know what's really going on in there. My interactions with the teacher are more limited. I get phone calls from her sometimes, but those are when my child has done something wrong. I see her in conferences and IEP meetings. That's when she gives me a list of my son's difficulties. Is she being picky? Is she singling my child out? Has she tried to help him when he needs it? Does she get mad at all the kids for stuff like this? Does she care about him at all, or does she feel like he's a burden to her? I can't tell. Sometimes she can be pretty good at doing that politician thing, too.

It's hard to judge the actions of people you don't know. My interactions with the school and district

staff don't always give me a lot of information to
go on. But my other sources do. My neighbor has a
list of complaints about the school a mile long. Her
child was in our teacher's class a few years back, and
you wouldn't believe what she did to him. She says
her kid has been scarred for life.

And I met a mom in the parking lot who told me
about the awful things that happened to her child.
No matter what the mother did, she was completely
disregarded by the principal. I asked some moms on
our local Internet message board about our district,
and the response I got was universal—I definitely
need a lawyer. They say there's no way I'm going to
get anywhere on my own, and if I don't get legal
help, my kid will definitely get overlooked.

Everyone knows that the latest therapy or teaching method is the only way our kids will ever learn,
but rumor has it that our district won't pay for it
because it's too expensive. I'm told that my school
doesn't care about our kids—it's all about the bottom line for them. They say the school won't admit
this, of course. They'll just make up excuses and lie
so they don't have to pay for anything extra.

Trust—It's all about trust. Do I trust you? Do
I trust the information you're giving me about my
child? I'd like to. It would make my life a lot easier

if I knew that you care about my child and are working as hard as I am to help him succeed. But trust doesn't grow in a vacuum. It grows through relationships—like the one between you and me. It's built piece by piece, with every interaction adding to or subtracting from it. Without getting to know you, I don't have a clue what you're doing or why. All I can do is try to guess from the information I do have.

19

I NEED TO PROVE MYSELF

T he first few times I spoke to the secretaries in our school's office, they didn't smile. They weren't rude; they were crisp, concise, and professional. They asked what I needed. If I wanted to talk to my child's teacher, I was told to send her an e-mail to make an appointment. If I asked to speak to the principal, they told me I had to make an appointment. To drop off my child's lunch, I was instructed to leave it on the counter, and they would have a runner take it to him during the next break. If I brought in my child's forgotten homework, they said they were sorry, but he would need to bring it with him to school tomorrow.

When I saw my child's teacher at "Back to School Night," she was very friendly. There were too many

people there for me to introduce myself, so when I saw her the next day in the parking lot, I caught her attention. Her expression changed just a little. Up came a mask—professional, polite, and guarded, her eyes saying, "Who are you, and what do you want?" After I told her I was the parent of one of her students, she relaxed a bit. Once she found out I was just saying hello, she relaxed a bit more. She was friendly then, but I still remember her initial wary look.

Boundaries. When I was new to our school, what I saw were boundaries. Cool, clear, and well defined. *We are the school, and you are not. We will let you in this far, and no farther. We are the ones who make the rules. Play by our rules, or we will shut you out.* That was the message. No matter how politely it was delivered or how nicely it was stated, each interaction underlined the rules. There might be a note in each school newsletter that asked parents to partner in their child's education, but at school it was always clear who controlled the partnership.

At the time, I didn't know why the lines between us were drawn so firmly. I came to you, eager and willing to help my child, and was surprised to find you so guarded. I didn't know then why you did it, why you drew boxes in the sand for parents to sit in—*do this, this, this, and no more*. It wasn't until I noticed your interactions with other parents that I began to understand.

One parent yelled at you because her child didn't do his homework. Another accused you of laziness because her child couldn't read—even though the parent never bothered to do the assigned reading with her child. A dad said the reason his boy was always in trouble was because you didn't understand boys. A mother came to a meeting drunk. A surprising number of your students' parents didn't come to meetings at all. One accused all the teachers in your school of disliking her child and lying to make her child fail. One flipped you off in the parking lot because you told her to move her car from the fire lane. Several bounced checks for the fundraiser, and one threatened a lawsuit because his child tripped on the playground and hurt himself.

Not all your parents were difficult. Most were fine, and a few were wonderful. But at the beginning of the year, you never knew how each of us would behave. Which of us would be the parents who helped their child overcome his difficulties, and which of us would blame his difficulties on you? Which of us would smother our children and prevent them from growing; which of us would never show up at all? Before you could reach out and let down some of your walls to let me in, you had to know what kind of parent I was.

When I was new to your school, I didn't know I had to prove myself and build my reputation—that my good behavior and attitude would help break down the walls between us, just as accusations and blame would build them higher. I didn't know that although your barriers were in place, they might not be set in stone. They might be preliminary, and my attitudes and actions were helping to decide if they stayed in place or not. Would my behavior cause you to reinforce them and shut me out? Or could I chip away at your walls day by day to help build the partnership my child so desperately needs?

Now I know. I know that when we first meet, it will take a while for me to prove myself. It will take time to convince you to lower your defenses and for me to demonstrate that I'll be a good partner in my child's education. But you need to know that at the same time you're evaluating me, I'm evaluating you. With each interaction, I note your expression, your voice, and your attitude. Are you welcoming me to your school? Really? Or are your requests for partnership just a public relations bit of fluff, designed to lull parents into thinking that you care? Upon meeting you, I can't look into your heart and guess your intent and character any more than you can guess mine. All I have to go on, as I hand my child over to you, is whether I think the smile on your face comes from your heart or is something you just paste on as part of your classroom decorations.

20
SOCIAL INTERACTION MAY BE DIFFICULT FOR ME

If my child has autism, there's a possibility I have some of the characteristics of autism, also. Having a child with autism doesn't automatically mean I'm on the spectrum, but it does increase the odds. I may have only one or two mild traits, which are not enough to warrant a diagnosis. But, they can still get in the way of you and I being able to communicate.

Just as my child's facial expressions don't always reflect what he's thinking, mine may not, either. You may not always be able to tell whether I'm content, angry, stressed, or sad, by looking at me. I may not show much emotion at all, or I may display different emotions than the ones I actually feel. For instance, if I'm nervous or overwhelmed, I may laugh, or I

may just shut down. It's not intentional, it's just the way my brain is wired. So, please, don't mistake my stony-faced silence for arrogance or think I'm strange if I don't respond the way you think I should.

I may not have the same understanding of social interactions that you do. I may not care for small talk or be good at it. When we meet, if I get right down to business, I'm not trying to be rude or hurry you. If I leave abruptly after we're done discussing what I want to talk about, I'm not dismissing you or trying to make you feel unimportant. From my viewpoint, we're meeting for a purpose. So when we've fulfilled that purpose, we're done.

If I have a foot on the autism spectrum, I may speak very bluntly or make statements or ask questions you think are a little odd. I may just be trying to find the logic in the situation at hand, without intending to give offence. However, you may not see it that way.

I won't always pick up on the subtleties of your social communication. For instance, if you feel it's time to end our meeting, don't think that looking at your watch, gathering your papers, or mentioning that it's getting late is going to clue me in on the fact that you want our meeting to end. Instead, tell me directly. "I need to leave in 5 minutes." That statement tells me how much time I have to finish discussing what I think is important and lets me know what your expectations are. While some parents might think it's rude that you're so direct, I'll probably appreciate it.

I may also not understand what you're trying to tell me if you use a lot of qualifiers. Sometimes teachers try to "soften the blow" when they tell parents things that might upset them. They use phrases like "seems to be," "often," "not quite," "tends to," and other qualifiers.

But if you say to me, "Sometimes your child does things that remind me of other children I know who have autism," I may not understand that you mean you suspect my child has autism and I should get him evaluated. I may attach no importance to your statement. After all, sometimes my child does things that remind me of a duck, but that doesn't mean he is one. Instead, tell me, "Your child acts like he might have autism. You might want to get him evaluated." While that may be a little blunt for your more social parents, it could be the best way to give me the information I need.

If social communication is difficult for me, I may be a little hesitant to talk with you. My conversations with people I don't know sometimes don't go well, and I won't know why. So I may not want to meet with you unless I really have to.

Or, I may have difficulty with particular types of communication. If my auditory processing is a little slow and I have a hard time interpreting what people mean according to their tone of voice, talking on the telephone might not work well for me. Our conversation might go better if we can meet face to face. For some parents on the spectrum, written communication (like e-mail or writing notes) may be easier, or it may actually be harder. Just like you have ways you prefer to communicate, so do I. If we're having a hard time connecting, ask me what communication method works best for me, just to be sure we're going about it the best way possible.

I may not be good at recognizing people by looking at their faces. My child may be face blind, and I might be, too. If so, it's hard for me to go into a meeting and have to figure out whom everyone is and what his or her role is in my child's education. It's especially difficult if they're people I've worked with before, who expect me to recognize them. Just because I've spent hours working with you in the past doesn't mean I can recognize your face. A round of introductions at the beginning of meetings is helpful, and some parents may appreciate it if everyone wears name tags. You can always ask me for my preference.

People on the autism spectrum are sometimes perfectionists and may hyperfocus on things. I might be a real stickler for details. And if my child is having a hard time, or if you and I are trying to resolve an issue, it might go right to the top of my priority list. I may want to meet with you to discuss it right now, even if this is an issue you don't feel is urgent. Or, if you make a mistake, such as an error in grading his math test, it may bother me until you correct it. The more your mistake affects my child, the more insistent I may get. If my insistence bothers you, it may help if you tell me when you expect to have the issue resolved. For instance, tell me, "I'll have grades updated by the start of school on Monday." But if you miss your deadline, don't be surprised if I bring up the subject with you again.

Change may not be easy for me. All parents of children with autism have a hard time when our children make transitions, but if I'm on the spectrum, these changes may be particularly difficult for me. If you think we need to switch directions with my child's education, it may take me a few days to get used to the idea. I may react poorly until I've had time to process all the information you've given me about why the change is a good idea and how the new situation will work. You can smooth transitions for me (and my child) if you make sure I know about them as early as possible. Tell me why the transition is happening, what the new situation will look like, and that if the change doesn't work for my child, necessary adjustments will be made. Having this information would be helpful for any parent, not just those on the spectrum.

If I'm an adult who is mildly affected by autism, I've probably gotten pretty good at controlling my emotions. However, there are a few of us who still can't regulate our stress well. If you and I are in a meeting and you notice I'm starting to get wound up, you might suggest we take a break. Five minutes and a chance to get a drink of water might be sufficient to allow me to calm down again. If not, it may be better to continue our meeting on another day. Most people have a hard time processing a lot of data, especially if it's information they don't want to hear about their child. It can be simply overwhelming. For a parent on the spectrum, it can be even more so. Our meetings may go better if you break up the "giving data" part and the "deciding what to do" part into two meetings. Make sure they are scheduled far enough apart to give me time to process the information you've given me and to deal with whatever emotions it may generate. Again, many parents would benefit from this approach, not just those on the spectrum.

I may be very intelligent. I may not necessarily be more wise or more able to function in the world than you are, but I may have a wide knowledge base. Having autism doesn't reduce my intelligence; in fact, it may increase my ability to collect and retain information. Many adults with autism are quite bright. As such, I may also expect that as a school-teacher, you should be at least as intelligent as I am. If you're teaching mathematics to my second-grader and can't answer questions about what I consider to be basic math (such as how to use imaginary numbers correctly in an equation), I may conclude that you're not "smart" enough to teach my child.

Don't let my intelligence fluster you or let my attitude make you angry. Some of the things I say may come across as rude. While it's possible that my rudeness is intentional, most likely, it isn't. It's probably due to having poor social communication skills on my part. That doesn't make it okay for me to insult you. But if you get angry, upset, or defensive when you talk to me, you're going to be less effective at getting your point across. Instead, show me any data you have to back up the statements you make. Make sure the data come from reputable sources, because I will likely question the validity of your data otherwise. Stay calm, stay on topic, and ignore anything I say that you find insulting.

If I'm an adult with autism, it's probable that when I was a child, no one understood why I acted the way I did. Autism education and awareness are relatively new and don't stretch back to when I was in third grade. When I was in school, teachers didn't know about my sensory-processing difficulties, my poor social understanding, my perfectionism, or my difficulty with transitioning. Instead, most of them thought my behavior meant I was defiant, weird, lazy, willful, stupid, or too spoiled by my parents. Their treatment of me reflected this misunderstanding. My classmates weren't too understanding, either, and few school personnel did anything about it when other children let me know just how much of a weirdo they thought I was. The adults' point of view seemed to be that if I just wouldn't act so strangely, the other kids would leave me alone.

My experiences growing up may color the way I look at educators now. You may say that you understand my child, but my teachers thought they understood me, too. If my child tells me one thing, and you tell me another, I will be more likely to believe my child than most parents are. And, I probably won't believe much of what his classmates say, either. You may have to work a lot harder to establish my trust than you do with other parents.

If I have some of the traits of autism, it might affect the way I communicate and work with you. I may have the same difficulties with social communication that my child does, and I may be more likely to see my child's side of the situation than to empathize with yours. That may make me a little more difficult to work with than other parents, but it does have its upside. If you can get past taking offence at the differences in our communication styles, I'm a great resource for learning how to understand my child.

21

WHY SOMETIMES
I DON'T TRY

I magine you are wealthy and just bought a small, private airplane. You hire a crew, plan your trip, climb aboard, and take off. Soon, you're soaring above the clouds, relaxing as you enjoy the scenery out the window. Then the flight attendant interrupts you. "Pardon me," she says, "but the pilot is having some difficulties. He'd like you to come to the cockpit."

Startled, you hurry forward. The pilot greets you with a warm smile and tells you in the most kind and respectful way that he's very concerned about your airplane. While it's a very nice plane, it just doesn't respond the way most of them do. It's sluggish and unruly and difficult to control. Its engines cut out occasionally, and it's flying erratically. He's tried

everything he knows to do, and still there are problems. All in all, he's very worried and is wondering if you have any suggestions, since it is your airplane.

By now, you would probably be very alarmed. Maybe even panicky. Assuming that you are neither a pilot nor a mechanic, you would probably have few immediate ideas that the pilot himself hadn't already considered. As you rack your brain for anything that might help, you notice the pilot and attendant strapping on parachutes.

"Is it that bad?" you ask. You hurry to the parachute storage compartment, only to find it empty— the crew has taken the only chutes on board.

"No, no, don't worry," the pilot says. "This is just a precaution. We're going to stay right here and help you for as long as we can. Now, what have you come up with?"

At this point, you have to make a decision. This is the same decision parents of children with special needs have to make almost every day their child goes to school. Given that you are in a perilous situation that is outside your control, and you've got little knowledge that might help you find a solution, what will you do?

You could start yelling at the flight attendant and pilot. After all, they've been trained for these situations, and you haven't. They've got years of experience flying airplanes. They have people they can call on the radio who know how to fix airplanes and how to land the plane if something goes wrong. They must have faced this situation before—what did they do the last time this happened? Did they abandon ship and leave their passengers and plane to crash and burn? For heaven's sake—this is their job! It's what they're paid to do. Why are they shifting that burden onto you?

Or, you could go into massive denial. You could tell the crew that you're sure the plane will be just fine. Your friend had a plane like this, and things always worked out for him, so they shouldn't worry. Maybe this type of plane just flies like this some-times—perhaps it was built this way. You could reas-sure them and leave it in their hands, then head back to the cabin. There's a fully stocked mini-bar there, and this panicky flight crew is really stressing you out.

You could panic. You could start screaming. You could become so overwhelmed by the situation that your good sense gives way to hysteria. The pilot and attendant wouldn't like it. They'd have to decide whether to push you out of the cabin so they could try a few more last-ditch attempts to save you and the plane, or to just to give up and bail.

Or, you could calm down. You could indicate your willingness to help in any way possible. You could start asking questions to get a better understanding of the airplane's difficulties, search the cockpit to find any relevant manuals, use your cell phone to find anyone on the ground who may have some idea how you can get out of the predicament, or volunteer to help check inside the maintenance access panels and see if anything looks out of place. Even though you are in a terrifying situation, you could make the best use of your skills and tools at hand to survive.

What would you do? Everyone decides differently. Their personality, confidence in their own abilities, willingness to face difficult situations, and control over their emotions all play a part in how a person responds, whether they are trying to survive a flight in a malfunctioning airplane or help their child with special needs get through life. A person's intelligence level and occupation play little part in how they deal with their own personal emergencies. I guarantee that teachers and administrators who find themselves on the other side of the conference table, listening to experts tell them things they never dreamed they would hear about their own child, react the same way everyone else does—with fear, anger, denial, and helplessness. Having these feelings is part of our human response to stress, even when they contribute nothing useful, and even when they lead to disaster.

So the next time you sit across the table from me and wonder why I'm not doing everything you think I could to help my child, know that it's probably not because I don't care. It may be that this is the level of my coping skills. I am doing all I know how to do to help my child, but I am also on my own journey of personal development in this situation. I may not get very far very fast; humans have a hard time changing their nature. But give me as many opportunities as you can and encourage the progress I am making. Because once you give up, once you jump from the plane and pull your ripcord, my child and I are completely on our own, without a chute.

22

I'M TIRED

I've been taking care of my child since the day he was born.

Until he was old enough to walk, I carried him wherever he needed to go. Then I began chasing after him. I had to be fast to keep him alive. I always had to be two steps ahead of him, because it would only take one moment of inattention, one mistake, one thing I didn't anticipate, for me to lose him forever. I had to snatch him before he jumped into traffic. I fastened our furniture to the walls so that when he climbed bookcases, the entertainment center, and the stove, they wouldn't topple over and crush him. I held him tight when we walked near water, animals, or fire. I installed locks on our doors and windows to keep him from escaping. The locks

worked until he was old enough to unlatch them. Then I prayed I had taught him enough to keep himself safe, because I couldn't anymore.

He went off to school, and the other kids didn't act like he did. The general-education teachers never expected that he would figure out how to get off the school grounds, so he could walk home. Or that he would go into the unlocked janitor's office and play with the cleaning chemicals and power tools. Or that he would climb into the back of a delivery truck while no one was looking. I couldn't keep him safe from himself while he was at school, and no one else could, either.

A path of destruction has followed him since he was able to move on his own. He pulled down curtains, took apart toilets, and dumped out purses whenever he could reach them. I apologized every-where we went. *I'm sorry he pulled your pictures off the wall. I'm sorry he dumped your lemonade out just to watch it spill across the table and onto the floor. I'm sorry he bit you, hit you, or climbed you like a tree so he could see what was in your pocket.* I replaced broken things, soothed hurt feelings, and spent too many days with my child in the emergency room. It's hard when you feel relieved that at least it was your kid who got hurt this time and not the other child, because otherwise, how could you ever face that child's parents again?

Always there were questions. From teachers and relatives and people on the street, in stores and at the bank. *Why did he do that? What's wrong with him? Doesn't he know better?* I tried to ignore the stares. The advice I politely listened to and then forgot about. *He wouldn't do that if you were more strict with him. He would learn to talk if you made him ask for things. Go ahead, let him loose to go play in there with the other kids. What's the worst that could happen? You should spank him. You'd never have gotten away with behavior like that when you were his age.*

The social events that we could skip, we did. I'm sorry, we can't go to your all-day wedding and reception at the beach, even if you've brought coloring books to keep the kids happy. Camping with our friends? With my child near a fire pit? And no walls to keep him contained? No. Not now, not ever. You want him to come to your child's birthday party? Where I have to watch all the other moms watch my child as he stands next to theirs, the kids who know that at a pool party you're supposed to go into a bathroom to change into your bathing suit and that if you don't like the cake you don't yell that it stinks and throw it on the floor? I'm sorry, but no, we won't be coming—not if wild animals dragged us there.

We quit going to church. I didn't want to, but we did. I could have used the support, but it was harder to go than to stay at home. We tried going a few times over the years, but we always decided my son wasn't ready. Every time we left him in the nursery, he screamed nonstop for the length of the service. When he was older, he demolished the Sunday school room and made the teacher cry. He announced to everyone that "God is stupid" for telling Abraham to kill his son on the mountain. At first, it was only the adults that looked at my child funny. But when the other kids started doing it too, I just didn't have the strength to fight that battle. School is mandatory, but we could opt out of church. So we did.

We've gone through a lot of testing, by teachers, psychologists, psychiatrists, neurologists, speech professionals, occupational therapists, and more. They listed and discussed all the difficulties my child has—anger, impulsivity, attention problems, aggression, immaturity, obsessions, muscular incompetence, and a lack of social understanding. We discussed each issue, one by one. We came up with examples and checked for patterns, and I had to admit out loud that my boy's behavior went way beyond normal childhood development. I felt like I had to prove that it wasn't my fault and that he was not spoiled, abused, or neglected at home.

Sometimes, the professionals listened and had answers. Sometimes they didn't. In those cases, it was up to me to search until I found someone who did, or, failing that, I had to figure out the answers on my own.

Various doctors gave us diagnoses: *autism, Asperger's syndrome, ADHD, pervasive developmental disorder—not otherwise specified,* or *unknown.* Medication was prescribed, and I had to decide whether the possible side effects of the pills outweighed the risks of my son not taking them. Weight loss and weight gain were relatively easy to deal with. Liver damage, less so. Self-injury and suicide were too painful to even contemplate. Each day that his challenging behaviors continued was dangerous. We got telephone calls from school to tell us about near misses with cars in the parking lot. He had a strong attraction to his dad's power tools, no matter how carefully we locked them up. *Choose,* each situation said. *Make a guess. Gamble that your child will live, while you experiment with his future.* I researched, prayed, and pondered, then gave him the medicines prescribed. Then I waited, and watched, and prayed some more. I recorded data. I had discussions with his doctor. I cried inside when we discovered that the medication we had chosen didn't work, and we needed to start all over again. We went back to the beginning and read about more side effects. We had no choice but to keep going, searching until we found something that worked, something that would bring my boy back from the edge and safely into our world again.

So far, we've survived, but our future lies before us, and it scares me. All the dangers we've faced we may have to face again, but now the consequences will be greater. My child will be on his own some-day. He'll have to deal with all that I've dealt with and more, and I don't know if I can get him ready in time. Can he curb his impulsivity, or will the attention he gives some pretty girl get him in trouble with the police? Will he wind up dead in a bar fight? Will he be able to hold a job? What about handling credit, debt, and taxes? Will he take care of his health? Will he be able to form a relationship with someone who will love him and help him through life?

That time is coming soon, and I don't have long to get him ready. I have so much to do and so little time to do it. If I make all the right decisions and find all the right resources, maybe I can make it happen.

Maybe I can help him develop enough skills to keep himself safe. But I'll have to work hard, and I can't afford to make mistakes.

We've done so much already, for so long, and we have a long way left to go. I need to be on top of everything, or the results could be catastrophic.

But I'm tired—I am so very tired. I'm trying to care as much as I did in the beginning, and I do. I care about my child more than words can say. But I just don't have the energy I used to. I don't know if I can make it to the end, until he doesn't need me any longer. I hope I can, but I just don't know.

23

I AM AFRAID

It is commonly said that grief drives the behavior of parents of children with special needs—the grief of what their child could have been and should have been, compared with what they are. For some families that may be true, but for most of us, what drives us is our fear.

As long as my child is with me, I can help him. I can remind him to calm down, slow down, and think before he acts. I can explain how our society works and run interference between him and the world when it's needed. When I'm by his side, I can remind him to look for cars before he crosses the street and to stay away from dangerous situations. I can make sure he apologizes when he needs to and accepts the consequences of his actions, even if

they're unpleasant. When something goes wrong, I can help him understand what happened and what to do instead in the future. When I am with him, I can help him navigate the world, and I can keep him safe.

But he's not always with me. He goes to school and other places I can't follow. He may be invited to another child's home, or we may have found an after-school activity he can tolerate and even enjoy. It's good that he goes without me. How can he learn to function on his own if I'm always there to take care of everything? How can he grow to be a man, if his mommy always protects him? But that doesn't mean it's easy for me.

I've had too many years of telephone calls from teachers and other children's parents. Some were calls of concern. Most were "informational," just letting me know that something had happened. Some were angry calls, demanding immediate action on my part. So far, I've been able to resolve whatever problems prompted the phone calls. I have apologized and explained; I have gone to collect my child and soothed whatever emotions he or the teachers, parents, or other children had that needed soothing. Sometimes, we had to make a trip to the emergency room for stitches or to the store to buy a replacement for whatever got broken. But I've always been able to bring my boy back to the safety of our home, so I could try to teach him a little more before sending him out into the world again. Then I waited for the telephone to ring.

Up until now, I've been able to keep my child safe, but that won't always be the case. It only takes one moment of inattention to make crossing the street fatal. It only takes one angry parent to decide that a comment my son made about his daughter's body constitutes sexual harassment. One poor decision can get him beat up or kicked out of school, or worse. My son is getting older, and the consequences of his actions are getting bigger. Behavior that in first grade would have meant a trip to the principal's office can mean a ride in a squad car by the time he reaches high school.

Has my child learned what he needs to keep himself safe? I've thought so before, and I've been wrong. In the past, there were times I thought we had reached a point of stability. I thought that if he hadn't learned to navigate the whole world on his own, then at least he had figured out how to deal with a particular part of it. Then I got a telephone call that proved me wrong.

When I'm with my child, I can take care of him. When I'm not, I can't. I fear those times. I fear them today, and I fear them tomorrow. I'm especially afraid of the day he decides he is old enough to leave my home forever. One bad decision is all it takes to create a situation I can't help him fix. Have I taught him enough that he'll be able to make it through life successfully? Will he be able to deal with the next thing the world throws at him? Have I taught him enough so that when I am gone, he can make a life for himself and be safe, happy, and loved?

I don't know. And it scares me.

24

DON'T GIVE UP ON US

Some days, I watch as my child screams his frustration to the world. Although I am calm as I help him, and I smile as I ignore those who gather to stare, inside I cry.

I cry because today is hard for him, and all the possible futures I see for him are hard, too. Social rules that make no sense to him will cause him to trip again, resulting in one misstep and perceived rudeness after another. How will he hold a job? Will he find a friend or someone to love him? Will he ever understand the connection between the words coming out of his mouth and the looks on the faces of the people around him? Will he someday be able to listen to what people say, look into their eyes, and read their hearts? If not, how will he

protect himself in this uncertain world or find the good that is also in it?

His passions rule him now: frustration, anxiety, curiosity, obsession, fascination, and rage. Waves of emotions rock him, rising from nowhere to flood his brain and take over his body, then slowly leaching away. He cannot control them. He cannot see them coming or ride them when they do. They rise and tear my sweet boy away from me, and he's gone yet again. Where will they lead him? For now, I can contain him in my space, but in a few years he'll be out of my reach and will go wherever his emotions push him, however unhealthy that place might be. For each good life I can imagine for him, I can conjure up 10 alternatives that haunt me.

Mostly, I cry because I feel I have failed him. We have worked on facial expressions and what they mean, but can you really teach someone to recognize a lie or to know when someone wants to be kissed? I can't. We have practiced controlling emotions—taking deep breaths, relaxing muscles, and thinking about things we like better than the here and now that can be so bothersome. Yet, here is my son before me, shrieking because life isn't the way he thinks it should be. Handwriting can be taught, and so can algebra. If I work hard enough, I can teach him any academic subject he needs to learn. But I cannot teach him normalcy—not even the parts he needs to survive.

I have worked so hard, for so long. I've had to struggle to become the parent I am today, and there is such a long journey ahead of me to become what I need to be for him. Some days I cannot see our path. I cannot see our progress—whether we are moving forward or backward or simply sinking. All my efforts may just be digging us further into the mud. We have no milestones or guides. There is no one to tell me if success is even attainable or what that success will look like.

Some days, I am lost, and I want nothing more than to sit down on the floor next to my child and shriek along with him. Or retreat into an easier life of denial, accusations, and delusions. Some days I want to give up because it feels like nothing I'm doing makes a difference. There is only autism until I die, and then he will have to face it on his own.

These are the days I need you. I really, really do. I need you to tell me you value my child, even when he's difficult to be around. I need you to show me the progress he's made and prove to me that all our efforts are inching us forward. Tell me that although he is shrieking now, he wasn't this morning or yesterday and that he's doing much better now than he was last month. Or that you can see why he's upset and you have an idea how we can help him learn to do better in this situation—if not tomorrow, then next week or next year. Point out to me the sweet child who exists behind the tears. Help me remember that he's still in there, still trying to emerge.

You can't fix the difficulties my child and I face. You cannot cure us or help us escape from the labyrinth of autism. You can advise us and perhaps lead us, but you can't propel my child and me any faster or further than we move on our own.

But when we stop, when I'm too tired and too weary and I can't see a way forward, when I want to sit down, give up, and sink into despair and failure, that's when your words have the most power. They become a lifeline that I can latch onto, a light that shows me the path to hope. It's true that while you cannot make me do the things I need to do, sometimes you can give me the encouragement I need to keep going.

Please, don't quit trying. Don't give up on my child, and don't give up on me. Some days, the only strength I have left is the strength you give me.

25

I LOVE MY CHILD

I love my child. More than the sun and moon and the stars and everything in between. As much as you love your children, and as much as you were loved as a child. As much as all children are loved, whether they are brilliant, slow, athletic, short, or tall, whether they like hockey or hate ballet. I hope for him as all parents hope. I pray my child grows to be happy and competent and able to follow his dreams. I want him to love and be loved. I hope he enjoys his life and finds meaning in it, whether the rest of us understand the meaning he finds or not.

I cherished his first step, his first word, and all the other firsts in his life. I celebrated them just as you did with your children, and as your parents did with you. We are lucky. There were more firsts for us

to recognize, firsts you may not have noticed when your children accomplished them. We celebrated the first time he ate a sandwich, because it meant he conquered some of the texture difficulties he has with food. We celebrated the first time he watched a movie in the theater instead of running screaming into the lobby because it was too loud. His first day at school with no tantrums was big. His first lie was important, because it revealed an understanding of the way someone else thinks. Making his first friend was special, and so was making the first friend he was able to keep. His milestones may have been different than your children's were, but they were victories just the same.

In spite of his difficulties, I love my child. I love that he still tries after so many failures. I love that he cares, even after experiencing so much rejection. His spirit and his heart are what matter most to me; the rest is just stuff to be worked on. Some of his difficulties cause him pain, and if I could change them, I would. I'd give my arms and legs and heart to give him the capabilities he'll need to make it in this world. But I can't. So instead, I'll have to use them to help him learn what he can. If that means I have to work, then I will work. If it means fighting battles, then I will fight. If it means facing the entire world and telling everybody they are wrong about my son, then I'll do that, too. Because I love my child.

From the very first time I held him, and his tiny hand wrapped around my finger and my heart, until now, as I watch him step away from me and struggle to do what is right, I love him. Now and for always, to the end of time and back again. Just as you love your children, and as you are loved. I love my child.

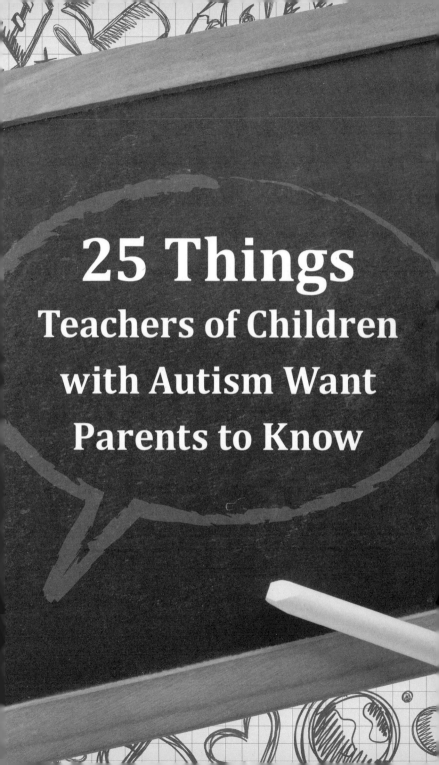

25 Things
Teachers of Children with Autism Want Parents to Know

1

I CARE ABOUT YOUR CHILD

Y ou have a wonderful child, and I'm glad to be part of his life.

Yes, he may have learning and behavioral difficulties. He may act a little oddly now and then, and he may need more of my attention than the rest of my students do. His obsessive nature may drive me to distraction some days, and his perfectionism may mean I spend a lot more time clarifying my directions and lectures than I normally do. He has challenges that may require me to rethink how I do things, so I can come up with something that works better for him. Your child may not be an easy student to have in my class, but that doesn't mean I don't like him.

I love that your child is passionate and has things he really wants to learn about. Whatever it is that catches his interest, whether it's common for kids his age or not, I love that he'll do research and learn all he can about it. It's wonderful that he wants to take trips to museums and exhibits, search the Internet, read books, and collect and classify samples. Your child's quest for knowledge is not something I see every day in my classroom, and I love it. Yes, sometimes I wish he cared more about what I was trying to teach him than he does about hubcaps or medieval siege weapons. It would make my life easier, and it would make his life easier, too. But, still, I love that your child loves learning.

I love that your child isn't cruel. Some of the things he says or does are rude. They may make sense to him, with his own understanding of the social world, but to the rest of the class, they come across as unkind. But I know that isn't his intent. Each year there are a few mean kids in my class, but he isn't one of them. He's not trying to put Hannah down for being chubby or promote his own social standing by pointing out that Jason doesn't play ball well. He's reporting what he sees, or he's reacting to his own frustrations. Do his limited social understanding and his difficulties with emotional control get him into trouble? Yes, they do. I need to smooth over plenty of hurt feelings, and I have to work to promote understanding in all parties involved. But I'd far rather work with a child who is trying to understand how to get along than one who's using his social understanding to intentionally hurt other people.

I love that your child tries. His school day isn't easy. He makes a lot of mistakes, and he has a lot to learn. Sometimes his stress and anxiety are overwhelming, but once he calms down, he comes back and tries again. He wants to do well in my class. He wants to have friends. He wants to be good and do the right things, and even though his challenges may make those goals harder for him to reach, he still keeps reaching. I admire that in him.

I like teaching your child, watching his expression when he learns something new, and helping him figure things out. I like watching him grow, take responsibility for himself, and discover the path he'll take in life. He doesn't always develop the same way or at the same rate as my other students, but his growth is just as important to me as theirs is. His milestones may be different, but they are accomplishments just the same, and I treasure them.

I want your child to succeed. When he struggles, I struggle. I try to find new ways to reach him. I go to trainings, read books, and talk to other professionals to try to find something that will help. I rearrange my classroom, bring in experts to observe us, try new teaching strategies and new materials, set up peer buddies, spend extra time with him, recommend assessments, talk to my administrators, and keep in touch with you. I give advice, and I ask for advice, too. I spend hours collecting data, implementing plans, and sometimes going back to the drawing board. I do it because I need to, because it's my job, but mostly because I care about your child.

When your child started in my classroom, he may not have been my "favorite kind of student." I may not have been trained to teach children with special needs or have expected that's what I would be doing. But now that your child is in my class and I've gotten to know him, I'm in his corner. I want to see him learn to cope with his difficulties. When he fails, I feel bad. When he succeeds, I celebrate. I brag about his victories to my colleagues and give them advice on how to help students with similar challenges. As I gain experience and confidence in working with kids with special needs, I'm willing to do more. I expect more from myself, other teachers, and our administrators. Your kid becomes one of my kids. My definition of my "favorite kind" of student grows to include yours. And I grow to become one of "his kind of teachers."

Are all teachers this dedicated? Will they all work this hard to help your child succeed? No, a few of us won't. Some of us are burned out or we made the wrong career choice or we really have no empathy for children who struggle. There are a few of us who shouldn't be teachers—just like there are a few parents who aren't up to raising children, a few doctors who don't make the grade, and a few engineers who really need to find another line of work. But most teachers, the vast majority of us, are here because we want to help children learn and succeed.

When your child comes into my classroom, I have an obligation to teach him. That's okay by me. That's why I'm here—I want to teach him. I'm waiting to see the lightbulb turn on, to watch his eyes when he learns something new. It will be only one of the many times in his life this happens, one of the many times he succeeds at what he attempts. It will be a minor victory in a long string of victories that make him who he is. But it will be my victory, too, and I want to be there to share it.

I care about your child.

AUTISM MAY BE
NEW TO ME

I may not know how to work with your child.

It's not because I'm dumb, stupid, lazy, unwilling, or uncaring. It's just that I don't know how. Until recently, teachers who wanted to work with students with special needs became special-education teachers. When they were in college, they took classes that taught them how to work with kids with challenges. They learned how to understand their needs, how to motivate them, and how to help them learn. The rest of the teachers in training, those who planned to be general-education teachers, didn't take those classes. They didn't have to. Students with special needs usually stayed in special-education classes, and typically developing students stayed in general-education classes. But, it's not like that anymore.

Now the boundaries are blurring. Our focus is less on "in which class does your child belong?" and more on "how can we support your child's needs?" Children aren't limited to attending only general-education or only special-education classes. Students can belong to either classroom or both, as their needs dictate. Kids with special needs can be mainstreamed into general-education classrooms for the whole day or for part of the day, to learn academics, socialization, or life skills. It's wonderful for the kids and for the teachers, and I'm all for it. Children need to be taught at the level at which they're ready to learn.

I'm all for including your child with special needs in my classroom. But if I'm a general-education teacher, I may not know how to do it successfully.

If your child has autism, it can be especially hard for me. Most general-education teachers haven't been trained to work with children with autism. School administrators, psychologists, and counselors are beginning to learn, but they have a long way to go. Special-education teachers have the skills but are likely to be most experienced in teaching kids who are moderately to severely affected by autism. Not many of us have been trained on how to teach mildly affected children, because until recently, most of us did not know the condition exists.

It used to be that if a student made noise in class after I told him not to, I figured it was because he was being defiant. A kid who hit another child was acting like a jerk. A student who cried all day was perhaps being babied at home by his parents, and a kid who argued with me about my rules was disrespectful. Back then, I acted on the information and training I had. Now we have even more information and insights than we did before.

If I've had training in autism, I'll know there are reasons why a child with autism may make noises, hit, cry, and argue. If I haven't had training, I may conclude that bad behavior on his part is to blame. A lot of children with autism don't appear to have special needs. Higher-functioning kids often have a great vocabulary, talk well, and are visibly intelligent. They may not look like they have developmental delays. To someone who doesn't know better, they could appear to be just acting difficult.

If I haven't had training in autism, I may not know how to work with your child. I may not understand his behaviors, and I may not know how to help him. But that doesn't mean I don't want to. I do, but it may take me a while to learn.

It also doesn't mean I'm a bad teacher. Over the course of my career, I've picked up a whole lot of tricks and techniques to help me teach children. Once I understand your child, I can use these teaching methods to help him, too. Once I know why he does what he does and how the world looks through his eyes, I can figure out how to help him learn in my classroom. I'll be able to gauge what I can expect from him, recognize his abilities, and determine which skills we need to help him develop. I can use what I know to help him succeed.

I may not have had the opportunity or a reason to get training in autism before, but if your child is in my class, I do now. When you were learning how to parent your child, having support was important to you. Now, having support is important to me. Have patience with me while I learn how to teach your child.

3

TEACHING METHODS

There are a lot of people trying to make money off of your child. They can spin a good story. Their product looks pretty in its box. They've got a Web site, with photos of smiling children and page upon page of testimonials to back up their claims. Whatever they're selling—cures, potions, powders, or reading programs—they've got proof it works. They've done studies themselves to prove it and will show you the results. Of course, they could have just made up the numbers, or they could have rigged the studies in their favor, or they could have only reported the cases where they got positive results. We only have their word that they didn't make it all up, and they'll make a lot of money if they can convince people to buy their product. Do you trust them enough to gamble your child's future on their claims?

There are also a lot of well-intentioned people out there who really do want to help your child but may not know as much as they think they do. Maybe they saw a special report on TV about autism and how you can cure it. Or, they may believe a teaching method must work because someone told them it would. Or they might think something that helped their child will work for yours, because all children with autism are the same, right? Or perhaps they really do want to help you, but maybe they just haven't done their research.

It's not easy for a parent to decide how to help their child. It's not an easy decision for schools, either. A lot of companies say they have the answer, that they're on the cutting edge of educational science, and that they've developed the greatest product ever. But this is your child's education. We need to help him now; we only have so much time to help him before he's done with school. So before we invest your child's time and energy and our money in a product, we want proof that it works.

That's why we start with methods that have worked well for us in the past. We have evidence that they are effective. While there is no guarantee they will work for your child, there is a good chance they will. We will try them first and see if we get results before we try something new and unproven.

Teaching students with autism is a new field, and we don't have a lot of data yet about the best way to do it. But once we understand your child, we can try things that have been successful with kids who are similar. Teaching kids with autism may be new to us, but we have taught children with obsessive-compulsive disorder before, and we can use what we've learned with them to come up with ideas to help your child deal with his perfectionism or anxiety. We've had students with learning disorders, attention disorders, and reading comprehension difficulties, and problems with organization and behavior. The children we've taught in the past may not have had autism, but they have had some of the same difficulties children with autism do. The methods we've developed to help them may help your child, too, and we have enough faith in those methods to try them.

If we need to, we will try new teaching methods and techniques, but we'll use ones with solid research behind them. We'll look for products that are backed up by data gathered by researchers who won't make money or otherwise profit if we decide to buy the product. We may also try methods that have been used by other schools with success or those from organizations who have produced other effective programs. If we're going to invest in a new program to teach your child, we're going to go with one we know has a good chance of helping him.

So, please understand that if we decide against trying a program or method you've brought us, it's generally because it either doesn't have enough reliable data to back up its claims or because we already have something we believe works just as well or better. It doesn't mean we don't care about your child, and it doesn't mean we don't want to spend the money to help him. We do. But we don't want to invest his time and our money on something if we're not relatively certain it will be effective.

Your child will be in our care for a very short time. We need to make the most of the time we have with him. If there's a teaching method or program we want to try with your child, it's because we believe in it. Let us try it. After a while, if we are not seeing results, we can come together, reevaluate our approach, and perhaps change it. Our goal is to help your child. Please let us use the best tools we have to do that.

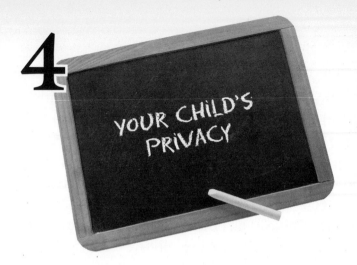

4

YOUR CHILD'S PRIVACY

I f your child was ill and his doctor didn't know how to help him, you'd want the doctor to do research. You would expect him to read medical books and look up current studies, but you'd probably also like him to ask advice from his colleagues and perhaps call in specialists. You'd want the doctor to do whatever it took to find out how to help your child.

When your child has a problem in my classroom, I'd like to have the same freedom to find a way to help him. I don't want to be limited to using the information I already have or can find myself. I'd like to be able to talk to other people who have the knowledge I need. There are a lot of resources at our school and in our district that can help, too. We have

teachers who are experienced in teaching kids with special needs. Our psychologist has insights into autism that can help me understand your child better. Administrators know what kind of supports, accommodations, and modifications are available that can make your child's school day easier and more productive. Occupational therapists, speech professionals, and adaptive PE teachers all have ideas that can help me be a better teacher for your child.

I understand that your child's privacy is important, and I know that it's necessary. I respect his privacy. I won't stand around in the teacher's lounge gossiping and complaining. I won't discuss him with other parents or with students, either. Your child's strengths and weaknesses are his business, as well as yours and mine—and nobody else's. That's not only common sense, it's the law. I will protect your child's privacy.

But, it's also important for me to be able to get help and information when I need it. It would be terrible to let your child struggle if there is someone in our district who can give us ideas that could help. If you insist that I never discuss your child's difficulties with other teachers and staff members, then you're taking away a lot of my resources. I may be a very good teacher, but that doesn't mean I know everything there is to know about teaching your child. Please don't limit my access to information that could help him.

You might also want me to talk to other people about your child if it will smooth the way for him. For instance, when he needs to go into another class-room for a while, his life will be a lot easier if the teacher there understands why he does what he does, especially if his behavior is much different from that of the other students. If he's working with a parent volunteer, understanding his behavior would help her work with your child more effectively. I'd like to be able to give the volunteer the information that's necessary for her to be able to help your child. That's it. There will be no gossip or in-depth discussion. I just want to relay the facts that will help others who work with your child understand and appreciate his strengths, learning styles, and needs.

In some instances, it may also be a good idea for me to talk to your child's classmates. If he does things the other kids think are odd, it may help if they know it's not because he's weird or being a jerk. If they know it's because he has difficulties, they may be more helpful and patient with him. Again, this doesn't mean discussing every little thing with his classmates—it means having a brief talk with them, so I can explain why and how your child needs help and the behaviors I expect from them as his peers. Sometimes it's not a good idea to reveal information about your child's difficulties to his classmates. It depends on your child and on the other kids. But, I'd like the option to be on the table, so you and I can discuss it and decide if it would help the other children to be more friendly and accepting of him.

Our main focus needs to be how we can best help your child. Gossip for the sake of entertainment certainly won't help him. But neither will limiting the information I can gather or letting him get a reputation as a "difficult child," when he's really a child with difficulties. Please let me share the information I need to help your child. I will do it carefully and with compassion. I will do it for his best interests only. I promise.

5

THE OTHER STUDENTS IN MY CLASS

Your child is important to me.

His physical safety comes first. It's my job to protect him. I need to keep him from harm from other students and adults, keep him safe if there's an emergency, and, in the case of illness or injury, make sure he gets the medical attention he needs until he's in your care again.

I also care about his academic progress. I need to make sure he's learning. Our curriculum moves quickly—we've got a lot to learn and very little time to do it. It's not like when you and I were children. Now our state's curriculum is crammed full; it's almost more than what we can teach in the days we have. Your child needs to keep up, or, if he's having difficulties, he needs to catch up as much as possible.

It's my job to help him do it. I need to make sure that by the end of the year, he's had the opportunity to learn everything he needs to be successful next year. If he gets behind now, it will be tough for him to catch up later. I can't make him learn the material, but I will give him the best chance I can for him to learn it.

His social development is important to me, too. It won't do him any good to be a genius who doesn't know how to get along with other people. My goal is to help him grow to be a good citizen—competent, knowledgeable, responsible, independent, and caring. I want him to be confident. I want him to be happy. I want him to know what he needs to be able to get by in life, to be able to follow his dreams and to make the world a better place.

I want all of this for your child. Because he's important. Because it's my job. Because I care about him.

I want all of this for my other students, too. Every child in my class is important.

Your child's classmates are just as important to me as he is. My responsibilities to them are just as great. I need to keep them safe; I need to make sure they learn; I need to help them develop. Some kids may need more help than others, but they all have needs. They all have potential, and they all have dreams. And they all need to be ready to meet the demands that will be placed on them next year. They are my responsibility—because they deserve it, because it's my job, and because I care.

This means that the student in my class who has dyslexia needs more of my attention, so she can learn to read. The child whose father is in prison needs my help, just to keep going. The kid with ADHD needs extra help to learn how to organize his desk, or he'll fail. The child who doesn't speak English well and the one whose parents are getting a divorce need my help, too. Your child needs extra attention, and I'll be happy to give him what I can. Just like I will for all of my students.

Sometimes, the needs of my students collide. Your child may be learning to "use his words" instead of hitting other people. That's a huge accomplishment. It's important, and I'll assist him with it as much as I can. But that doesn't mean I can let him learn that lesson in my class if he's attacking other students, threatening them, or making them feel persecuted. I can't let them hurt him, and I'm not going to let him hurt them, either. My first responsibility is to keep everyone safe. Social lessons come second. This doesn't mean that if we decide to move your child from my class, I won't ever let him come back again. Once he's learned better self-control, I'd love to have him come and try again.

Also, we can't allow your child's behavior to prevent the other kids from learning. Little disturbances here and there are okay. Sure, a student isn't supposed to blurt out in class, but we can work on that throughout the school year. Occasional minor comments here or there won't slow down my teaching that much and won't get the other students too far off track. Depending on your child's age, we might be able to deal with an occasional screaming fit, too. If keeping quiet in class is a skill your child needs to learn, I'd love to help him learn it. But if his fits or outbursts are severe enough that they prevent me from teaching or they keep the other students from learning, then we need to do something different. The other children have the same right to an education that your child does. If they don't learn in my class this year, what will happen to them next year? Should they fail? Is your child's future more important than theirs?

I like your child. I like having him in my class, and I want him to succeed here. I want my other kids to succeed, too. I will help your child as much as I can, but I won't do it at the expense of my other students.

6

CAN I TRUST YOU?

There are horrible stories going around the teaching world about how some students with disabilities have totally disrupted classrooms. Not all the stories are true, but, unfortunately, a lot of them are, and that worries me.

I know a teacher who had a student with autism in her class. He screamed all year long. Day after day, he threw tantrums that lasted for hours; he couldn't be soothed, and the meltdowns never stopped. The teacher tried everything. She learned all she could about autism and consulted numerous experts. Nothing she tried helped him calm down. He was a child with a lot of anxiety, and that classroom setting was too stressful for him. It was the wrong placement, and all it did was make him miserable. He was

placed there because his mother insisted. She didn't want him to be in a special-education classroom "with all those weird kids." She said if we put him in a general-education classroom with typically developing children, it would help him learn to be "normal." It didn't. In fact, all it did was overload him. He had a horrible year, and so did the other students in his class. No one learned much of anything—not the boy with autism or his classmates. Everyone in the class had a terrible year, including the teacher.

Another friend of mine pulled her typically developing daughter out of public school because of a child with special needs. He hit her frequently. He pinched her and kicked her and flipped up her skirt. His mother said it was because he liked the girl and wanted to interact with her, but he didn't know how. The school had a behavioral plan in place and was working with the boy to teach him not to hurt people. My friend understood, but she wasn't interested in her daughter being used as a training tool. After a few months of it, she moved her daughter to a private school, where there were no kids with special needs.

One of my colleagues had a student with mild autism in her class. He was a sweet kid. The teacher liked him and was willing to work with him. But the kid wanted to be the class clown, so his classmates would like him. So he showed off—all day, every day. He told jokes and sang songs and gave really, really long rambling speeches. Because of it, there was no learning going on in that classroom. The teacher had a chat with the kid's mom. The mom told her son that he'd better straighten up or she'd homeschool him and make him work twice as hard. The child got more serious about school really quickly. He still blurted out during class and needed a lot of reminders, but when the teacher told him it was time to stop talking, he did. That student ended up doing well that year, and although he was a little disruptive, he no longer prevented the other kids from learning. It didn't have to work out that way; the year could have been much different. The mom could have told the teacher to just deal with her son's behavior, because he had autism and that's the way he was. Other parents have done it.

There was one student I had who was a real challenge. He was a great kid, but he didn't handle frustration well at all. He hit kids on the playground, ripped up the plants in the planter boxes, tore up his class work, and ran out of the classroom. His mom said he never did things like that at home. She said she would take him to doctors to get some ideas on how to help him. She said she would discipline him at home, so he would learn that he couldn't hurt people or tear things up. She said she might try giving him medication. She said a lot of things. Maybe she did them. But when she and her boy were talking to me, I never saw her act upon what I told her about his behavior. She said she was sorry, but I never saw her turn around and talk to her son about it. There was never any sign that she was doing anything to help her son learn self-control. She did tell me that his behavior was part of his disability. She told me that all year long, and his behavior never changed. Now he's a few years older, and I hear that his behavior has gotten even worse. Now no one wants him in their classroom. It breaks my heart, because underneath it all, he's a good kid. Maybe things wouldn't have turned out differently, no matter what his mom did. But maybe they would have.

There's a very nice student in my class who has a hard time reading. He can do it, but it's a struggle. His mom has been demanding that we do something. We have a reading program that gets good results, but his mom refuses to let us try it. Instead, she wants us to send her son to a very expensive reading school. Now there's a legal battle going on. His mom says she's fighting because her child is so important to her, but when I asked if they were doing the 20-minute reading homework each night, she said "No." She said she doesn't have the time. Every day in class, I'm doing all I can to help him, and yet I watch him fall farther and farther behind.

Now you're asking for your child to be placed in my class. He's got special needs and a few behavioral issues, and he struggles in some areas. I don't know your child, and I don't know you. I'd like to be open and inclusive and give your child a chance. I'd like to help him succeed. But I'm nervous—mostly about you. If this isn't the best place for your child, will you insist that he stays? Even if he hates it? Even if it's bad for the other students? Even if he's not learning anything and he is missing an opportunity to be placed in a classroom environment where he will learn? Will you put your child's needs ahead of the needs of the other children in my class? If you tell me you're going to do something, are you going to follow through? Will you support your child and help him succeed, or will you put all the blame for his difficulties on me? Will I spend all year haggling with you as I try to get him the help he needs?

I'd like to help your child. I really would. But until I get to know you, I don't know if I can trust you. You're asking me to take a risk. If I accept your child into my class, am I going to regret it later? Can you promise you'll try to make his year in my room work? Or will your child's story turn into another legend that floats around the teacher's lounge and makes everyone afraid to teach kids with special needs?

That decision is up to you.

7

WHAT KIND OF PARENT ARE YOU?

Almost all the parents I've worked with have been great. They support their kids. They make sure they do their homework. They keep their children fed, get them to bed on time, and give them the love and encouragement they need. If there's something they're unsure about, they ask. If there's a problem, we resolve it. Their children have a much better chance of learning what they need to know, because their parents and I work as a team.

Then there are the other parents—the ones who aren't so great to work with. There aren't too many of them, but I've had their kids in my class, and so have my colleagues. These are the parents who don't believe that when it comes to educating a child, there

are three responsible parties: the child, the parent, and the teacher. If their child isn't learning, they think the only person to blame is me.

I've had parents who didn't check on their child's homework, then yelled at me because the homework didn't get done.

I've had parents who complained when their child earned a bad grade. They have said he flunked because I'm lazy, sexist, racist, boring, incompetent, stupid, too old, too young, untrained, or a lousy teacher. They've said I'm out to get their child because I just don't like him. Sometimes they say that all the rest of the school staff and students are out to get him, too.

Parents have accused me of being mean to their son because I "just don't understand boys." I've taught hundreds of students, and half of them have been boys. Half the kids in my class now are boys, and, yet, their child is the only one getting into trouble. But, according to those parents, it's not their child's fault. It's mine.

I've had parents insist that their child had learning problems when he clearly didn't. The kid was fine. He got Bs and Cs, but those weren't good enough for Mom. If he wasn't getting As, there was something wrong, and I needed to fix it.

I don't tell kids they can't swear anymore, because I've had parents scream at me for telling their kindergartener he couldn't say the "F" word. So now I tell my students not to swear *at school*.

I've had parents avoid me. They disregarded the notes I sent home and didn't return my phone calls, and, if I finally got them to agree to a meeting, they didn't show up. That's happened more times than I can count. But, according to them, their child's difficulties were still my responsibility.

Sometimes, when parents have come to meetings, I wish they hadn't. Those are the times they have yelled at me, filed lawsuits, thrown things at me, threatened to have me fired, knocked over the table, broken things, or attacked me. One mom threatened me and told me she knew where I lived and where my children went to school. We've had to get restraining orders against parents. Sometimes they go to the newspaper and tell them how awful we were to them and their child. We can't tell the reporters anything different—in fact we can't comment at all, because it would violate the child's right to privacy. Parents have mentioned me by name in the paper and have accused me of all kinds of horrible things that weren't true. The newspaper people seemed to think it made a great story.

Moms have come to volunteer at school half-naked, in tight, short exercise clothes, or with shirts cut ridiculously low. Some schools I know have had to implement dress codes for parents.

Parents have come to school drunk or on drugs. A bus driver I know got punched when he wouldn't deliver a young student to a noncustodial parent because she didn't have identification. We've called the cops on a parent who was a known sexual predator and wasn't supposed to be near his kid or the school. We've had so many checks bounce that we don't take them anymore. We've had young kids from wealthy families come to school hungry because their parents never got around to feeding them. We've had parents with mental illnesses who were doing their best but were still a little scary.

Most of our parents are wonderful. Almost all of them are. But, a few aren't. When you come into my classroom for the first time, I assume you're going to be fine to work with, but I might be a little wary until I know for certain. Treat me with respect. Be responsible and help your child. Show me that you're not a problem parent. Then I'll know for sure that you're one of the great ones.

8

YELLING
NEVER
WORKS

If you were on the job and someone yelled at you, would you like it? If your boss yelled, would you work faster or better? If your colleague or your customer raised his or her voice, would it change your performance? If your husband, your child, or a stranger screamed at you, how would you react?

Some parents think the way to deal with teachers is to yell at us. They think it helps. It doesn't. It doesn't scare me or motivate me. It doesn't make me want to help your child more. It doesn't prove that you're a "serious, take-charge kind of person." It doesn't change your child's difficulties. It just makes you look like a jerk.

Yelling at me doesn't change my mind about your child, either. It doesn't make me like him more (it also doesn't make me like him less). I already want to help your child. That's what I do. That's why I'm a teacher. But, yelling at me does make me want to avoid you. If you're rude, unpleasant, or mean, I'm not going to want to talk to you. That's just human nature. No one, anywhere, wants to work with someone who's abusive.

Some parents think their child gets a reputation in the teacher's lounge—that if their kid has difficulties, teachers won't want to have him in their class. While that happens sometimes, it's not common. Each year, when students are divided into classrooms, schools try to balance the loads on teachers and build workable classes. There are quite a few kids with difficulties in every grade. I know each year that I'm going to get several kids who are having a hard time. I'm okay with that; it's part of my job. I don't mind helping kids learn to deal with their challenges.

Parents are the ones who get reputations. If your child has difficulties and has been at my school for a while, there are probably stories floating around the coffee room about you. If you're a great parent who supports your child and his teacher, I'll hear about it.

If you get involved, stay in contact, support us from home, and follow through by doing what you say you will, then all those great things you've done in the past will be remembered. If you're *not* great to work with, I'll hear about that, too. Remember that time you lost your temper because your kid didn't win the science fair? Everyone's heard that story. Do you recall the incident 4 years ago, when you threatened to file a lawsuit because you didn't like your child's grade? Oh, yes. That story will follow you the whole time your child attends our school.

Your reputation is something you build each time you interact with anyone at the school—the lunch ladies, the secretaries—everyone. It's one of your greatest assets. A good reputation opens doors and makes people want to help you more. Your child needs an extra few days on his homework because he worked his hardest but couldn't get it done? If I know you and your kid are hard workers who are trying your best and that you don't lie to me, I might give you the extra time. But if I think you're someone who doesn't follow through on things, I'll figure that your actions are teaching your child that it's okay for him to put off his work. I'll decide that the best way I can help him is to hold him accountable and help him learn the importance of managing his time, by showing him it doesn't pay to procrastinate. Your reputation helps me decide the best way to help your child.

It's not too often I hear a teacher say they don't want a child placed in their class because he's going to be trouble. That's pretty rare. More often, they say that having the child will likely be tough, but the parents are great, so they're willing to do it. A good parental reputation carries a lot of weight with us. It means we'll have a fair chance of helping your child. Of course, sometimes it goes the other way. I've heard teachers say they don't mind the student, but they don't want him in their class because his parents are just too much trouble. It doesn't happen very often, but it's pretty sad when parents become a liability to their child.

You wouldn't like it if people yelled at you. Please don't yell at me. The number-one reason teachers quit teaching children with special needs is not the kids. They love the kids and love working with them. The number one reason they quit is they can't stand being harassed by parents anymore.

9

LEGAL HELP

ake sure you've tried everything else before you seek out an attorney, an advocate, mediation, or a due process hearing. I'm not saying you should never get legal help. There are times when it may be the only thing that will get your child the help he needs. Really, honestly, and truly. But, those times don't happen as often as you might think, and there's a price that goes along with the legal process—one that has nothing to do with money. So before you go that route, make sure you've tried all your other options. It will be worth it in the end.

If you bring a lawyer or advocate to the table, it will change your relationship with us. It's hard to operate as a team if we're in the middle of a legal

battle. You'll be drawing a line in the sand that says "Us" and "Them." It means you're done working with us, that you're not interested in compromise or trying new solutions. You've decided what you want, and you're going to try to force us to give it to you, whether we think it's in the best interest of your child or not.

Bringing a lawyer or advocate into the room tells us that you don't trust us. It means you don't believe what we're telling you and that you think we're not trying to help your child. You think we're trying to cheat you and your child, or you think we're idiots. That can put a bit of a damper on our relationship. It may also make us wonder if we can trust you, too.

If you begin the legal process, we're going to start being more careful about bringing new solutions to the table. We won't be as open to trying things to see if they help your child. What if we try something and it doesn't work? Will you file for due process? Or will you insist that we keep doing it and file if we don't? Parents have done it in the past. Is the risk of going to trial worth it to us to try and help your child?

If you're filing for due process to get something we don't think is good for your child, we've got to decide if it's worth a fight on our part. Do we spend the time, money, and anxiety a hearing brings if we believe that what you're asking for will delay your child's learning? What if we know it won't help, but it will cost money that could go toward helping other kids? It might be easier for us to just give in, but is that what's best for everyone in the long run?

The threat of a due process hearing also means we have to be incredibly careful to follow every detail of the law—even the regulations that limit the advice we can give you about what might help your child. Any advice or tips and tricks we may have offered you in the past will stop, because we will have to be so careful now about what we say and how you take it.

We'll also have to spend extra time checking every last detail of your child's paperwork. If we make a mistake, even a typo, we could end up in court. Depending on my job description, I may be involved with hundreds of IEPs a year. That can translate into thousands of pieces of paper. I know each one is important, and I work hard to make sure they're all correct, but I'm still human. I'm going to make the occasional mistake, and I'm grateful if someone points it out so I can correct it. But I'd really rather it wasn't your lawyer pointing it out during a due process hearing. One time I pushed the wrong button on my computer during an IEP meeting and accidentally deleted a page of notes. The team and I rewrote them as best we could, but we ended up in due process anyway. If the parent had come in and worked with us, we could have rewritten the notes right away, but instead she decided to call her lawyer.

If you take the legal route, you'll limit the number of people who will want to work with your child. File against this year's teacher, and next year's teacher will assume there's a good chance it will happen to her, too. Some people who file against the school only do it once to fix a big problem, but some do it repeatedly for every little thing. Nobody wants to work with parents like that. That can be a real problem if your child has several years left at our school.

Due process hearings are also expensive—for you, for the school, and for all the rest of the students in special education. Money is tight. Spending it on necessary legal fees or services is one thing. Spending funds on frivolous cases robs other kids with special needs of money that could have gone to helping them. Make sure that what you're filing for is worth it.

Again, I'm not saying there are never times a parent might need a lawyer or advocate. Sometimes people do. Just know there are consequences for bringing one in. Weigh them against the benefits and make sure you've tried everything else before you head off to trial.

If you've got a problem, talk to your teacher. You'd be surprised how many parents don't. If the two of you can't resolve the issue, go meet with your principal. A chat with her can iron out most problems that crop up at school. If that doesn't work, try calling your school district. Make an appointment to meet with the person who runs the special-education department. Don't worry that you may make someone angry for going over his or her head—you won't. You're just making use of all the help that's available to you. Sometimes people at the district level have more resources than a particular school does, and often they can help everyone come to a good solution. If, after meeting with everyone, you're still having difficulties, talk to the superintendent of the school district. If you talk to her and are still unhappy, you can make your case to your school board. Don't listen to your neighbor's friend, who says your school district stinks and never helps anyone. Talk to them yourself and see what they can do.

If all else fails, you do have the right to get a lawyer or advocate and go to mediation or file due process to get what you need for your child. Most problems parents face with their child's school can be solved by talking to the right teacher or administrator, or the issues are minor enough that they don't warrant legal help. But if what you are facing is big and you've tried absolutely everything else, the legal route may be a good idea. Just remember that once you bring in lawyers or advocates, you significantly change your relationship with the school. Make certain you've exhausted every other avenue before you do.

10

SERVICES, ACCOMMODATIONS, AND MODIFICATIONS

Your sister's friend has a kid with the same diagnosis your child has. His school gave him speech therapy, occupational therapy, and time in the learning lab to help him with his homework. Her kid got those services, and now she's telling you that your child should get them, too. And if the school doesn't want to give them to you, it's because they don't care about your child and they just want to save money. So you'd better get a lawyer and sue the school—otherwise your kid will never, ever get any better, and you will be responsible because you wouldn't fight for him. She's got the name of a great lawyer, or she says you could use an advocate. They're both expensive, but they're worth it because this is your kid's future we're talking about. You don't want to mess this up.

She's right. You don't want to mess this up. We don't want to mess this up, either.

I'll admit it—there are a few schools out there that deny services to kids who need them just because the school doesn't want to pay for them. There aren't a lot of schools like that, but they do exist. If your child attends one of them, you'll need to fight to get what he needs. But that's rarely the reason schools deny services.

One reason services are denied is that there are still some schools out there that don't know enough about autism to know how to help your child. For example, they may not be aware that speech goals include the ability to carry on a conversation or that occupational therapy may improve your child's behavior in the classroom. If your school staff and administration haven't had enough training in autism to know what help is typically considered, it might only take a polite request to the head of the school district's special-education department to fix the situation. Remember that "not knowing" isn't the same as "refusing to help."

That being said, lack of awareness about autism is not the most common reason schools don't administer some of the services parents request. It's not that we don't care about your child, and it's not that we don't know what to do—it's that we don't think the services you're requesting are what your child needs.

Services are extra instruction we provide to students to meet their educational needs. For instance, if your child's speech is poor, he may need speech class, or if he's physically awkward, he may need adaptive PE to teach him basic motor movements. *Assessment tests* are one of the measurements we use to figure out which services your child may need. *Accommodations* (or *adaptations*) are ways we make it easier for him to function in the classroom without changing the work we expect him to do. We might assign him a front-row seat, or, if reading is hard for him, we might give him his textbook on a CD. *Modifications* are when we change our academic requirements. We could assign fewer homework problems, give your child a different final project, or grade his papers on a different scale. Services, accommodations, and modifications are provided to keep the student in the class where he'll learn best, give him the tools he needs to learn there, and help teach him the skills he'll need to survive in the adult world.

Each child is different. That's why we have the assessments. Just as students with physical disabilities have different needs, so do students with Down syndrome, autism, learning disorders, dyslexia, and other difficulties. We can't lump kids together because they have the same diagnosis. Some people with autism have poor muscle tone and control, and others are natural-born athletes. Giving all kids with autism adaptive PE would not only waste money, it would frustrate the athletic kids and waste their time. They'd be better off in regular PE, learning the social skills they need to get along there. Automatically giving children services because of their diagnosis would be the wrong thing to do, for the kids and for the school.

Assessment tests and input from the child, parents, and teachers help determine what kind of services, accommodations, and modifications would help the student reach his goals. We work on academics, social skills, and life skills. Math, English, and other academic subjects are not the only important things for him to learn—we also want him to learn skills that will help him be able to keep a job and function in life. We need to keep social and life skills in mind too when developing his program.

Sometimes, figuring out how to help your child meet his goals gets complicated. If he's having a hard time with math, first we have to determine why he's having problems. Is it because his math skills are below grade level? Is it because of organizational problems or attention difficulties? If he doesn't understand something right away, is he getting frustrated and either quitting or throwing a fit? Is he having problems reading the book or the board, or is he having a hard time listening to the teacher? Just because he's struggling in math doesn't automatically mean that extra tutoring is going to help. We need to figure out *why* he's having a hard time before we can figure out what supports or plain old teaching tricks are going to help him most.

We also need to be sure to deliver that help in an effective way. For instance, having your child visit the occupational therapist once a week may be useful. But, would it be better instead to have the therapist consult with the teacher and show her how to incorporate your child's therapy into his workday? For example, if what he really needs is to have an ongoing sensory diet, spread throughout his school day, then getting therapy once a week isn't going to help much. It would be better for him if his therapist kept an eye on how he was doing and helped his teacher provide what he needs in the classroom and on the playground. But if he needs to learn a particular skill, like how to hold a pencil or use scissors, perhaps direct teaching by the therapist is best. Or, your child may need a mixture of both methods—time spent in direct therapy and changes implemented in the classroom. All three options are valid ways to provide occupational therapy, but not all of them help all students equally. Part of deciding which services would help your child the most involves figuring out *how* to provide the services we give him so that they work.

Just because your child and the one down the street share the same diagnosis doesn't mean they need the same type of help. A good school program is built for your individual child. If you're passionate about getting him the help he needs, make sure you're not demanding something that's going to waste his time. He doesn't have a lot of time to waste.

11

I DON'T HAVE A MAGIC WAND

I wish I had the power to "fix" your child. I really do.

If I had a magic wand, I could make all my students' difficulties melt away. Dyslexia would evaporate. Autism would dissolve. Learning difficulties, mental disorders, and physical disabilities would all disappear. I could make my students happy and successful. I could change their brains, bodies, and personalities, so learning would be a breeze and coping with life would be simple.

If I had the ability to do that, I would—every day and with every kid I come across. My life would be easier, and so would theirs. Who wouldn't want to snap their fingers and fix all their students' problems?

Too bad life doesn't work that way.

If your child has difficulties, he might have been born with them, or he might have acquired them. However he got them, he has them now. And it's not in my power to make them go away, no matter how much I'd like to.

I cannot make your son become socially adept. Right now, science has no tool that can do that. I can help him learn some ways to act that will make his life easier. I might be able to help him replace some bad habits with better ones. I can do my best to explain to him why other people do the things they do and help him understand why this is important for him to know. But I can't physically grow the part of his brain that handles social interaction.

I can't cure your child of ADHD. If his attention wanders, then it wanders. I might be able to teach him some methods to stay organized and get caught up on his work, but nothing I can do will change the fact that he has ADHD.

If your child has a learning disorder, I may be able to help him find a way to work around it—I can give him some tools and study techniques and allow him to use machines that can help get information into or out of his head. But I can't make the disorder go away. He will still have a learning disorder when he leaves my class.

I know you get frustrated sometimes. You might think there must be some way for your child to cross over into typical development and that I'm just too stupid, lazy, or mean to do it. I wish that was true. Really. Then, if I just changed my behavior, your child would be fine. Or, you could get a new teacher, put him in a new school, or do something different, and your kid would be cured. Wouldn't it be great if life really worked that way?

But it doesn't. I can't change your child, no matter how much I want to help him. If I could, I would have done it already. If you could, you would have done it, too. If your child has difficulties, he had them yesterday and he will still have them tomorrow. We can't change that. But if we work together, we may be able to help him succeed, given the particular set of difficulties he has.

That's something we *can* do.

12

ASSESSING
YOUR CHILD'S
PROGRESS

There is no road map for helping your child. There is no guidebook that says if your child has this diagnosis, and we follow these steps and do these treatments, then everything will work out fine. There isn't a set of instructions for parents, and there isn't one for teachers. Each child is unique, and so each learning path is unique. What works for one child won't necessarily work for another. Students have different strengths, weaknesses, interests, and goals. To help each child, we must build individual plans to meet his or her needs. That's what an IEP is all about. It's a plan built especially for your child to help him reach his particular goals.

While we don't have a guidebook, we do have resources. We've got a collection of techniques and

strategies that have worked for us in the past, like a huge toolbox loaded with the tools of our trade. It's filled with our experience and knowledge, teaching methods, people we can call for advice and new ideas, and products we can try if we find that what we're doing isn't working. Some of the tools are standard ones we're currently using, like our math tutoring program, speech articulation class, and reward charts. Some are new and evolving, like our techniques for teaching social skills. And some are our old and trusted standbys. They may have been around for a while, but they've worked well for us before, and we still pull them out occasionally when we need them.

We know our tools. We've studied them and have been trained to use them. When it's time to put together a plan for your child's education, we work together with you to come up with his goals. Then we sort through our tools and figure out what we think will work. Which teaching methods and services do we think are going to help him reach his goals? We can't tell for certain how effective each one will be; every child is different. We have to make our best guess, create a plan, and try it out.

After we've implemented the plan for a while, we check to see if we're getting good results. Since we know our tools and know a lot about your child, we can evaluate how he's doing. Is he progressing as fast as we think he should? Are these tools working? Are there other teaching methods that would work better? On the basis of what we see, we can then decide how to adjust your child's plan to help him best.

Parents are a vital part of this process. You are part of the team that makes up your child's education—him, you, and us. Student, parents, and teachers. You know your child better than we do. You are helping to determine his goals and assisting him in reaching them. You're also evaluating his progress as we go along. Is he making improvement? Is it as fast as it could be? Is the school doing what it's supposed to be doing? Do we know what we're doing, or are we just wasting your child's time and patience? These are important questions. Unfortunately, as a parent, sometimes you don't have all the information you need to come up with answers.

Part of the problem is that most parents don't know a lot about childhood development with regard to education—meaning what skills typically developing children have at different ages. Unless parents have raised other children or been around a lot of them, they may not have a good measuring stick when it comes to evaluating their child's abilities as compared with those of other kids his age. If he's struggling with reading comprehension in the third grade, is it because he's got a problem, or is it because the class is reading more complicated material, and a lot of his classmates are having to work hard to keep up, too? If parents don't know exactly what's expected of their child at this age, how can they tell if his progress is satisfactory or not? We're aiming for at least average. But if parents don't know what average is, how can they tell if their child is getting there?

Another problem parents face is that they often don't know a lot about the tools we're using. They don't know how our programs and techniques work and what can be expected from them. For instance, children with autism typically have poor social skills. They have a hard time communicating, making friends, and interpreting other people's motives and intentions. As teachers, we've studied how to teach social skills. We have books, programs, tools, and experts to help us teach social skills to your child. But social skills are very complex. Learning them is a lifelong process, even with the best of help. To be socially adept, you have to recognize an almost infinite array of facial expressions and body language, to interpret what other people mean when it doesn't match what they say, to know thousands of unwritten rules about what is acceptable behavior and what isn't, to control your own emotions even when you feel them strongly, to know yourself well enough to recognize what will make you happy, and to know when your happiness isn't the most important consideration. Learning social skills is hard. So is teaching them.

Many of the skills we teach your child are not simple. We expect it will take a while for him to learn them. That's okay. But if you have different expectations, you may think we're not making enough progress, and you may become unhappy or angry. If you think receiving a school year's worth of social skills lessons will make social interaction easy for your child, you're going to be disappointed. We may be making good progress with the methods we're using, but if you have a different set of expectations, you won't see it that way. At best, this means the relationship between you and me will be damaged. At worst, it means you may decide to pull your child out of a program that is working for him, to try something that may not work as well.

The way to combat these problems is by communicating. If you aren't sure if something is working and that your child is making progress, come talk to me. Tell me your concerns. Ask for my opinion. Make sure you understand your child's goals and what he needs to learn to meet them, as well as how the tools we're using work and what we might expect from them. Make sure you have the information you need to evaluate his progress. Arrange a meeting, and I'll be happy for us to review the plan and evaluate it together. Then we can decide if we need to make some changes.

It's not easy to figure out the right path when educating a child with special needs. If all students were the same, maybe we could come up with a one-size-fits-all package. But they're not. That's why you and I have to tailor a plan to fit your child. It may need adjusting, and we may need to work on it a while, but it's worth it to come up with one that helps him.

13

WHY I TELL YOU THINGS YOU DON'T WANT TO HEAR

If I tell you your child is having difficulties, believe me. I am not telling you this to make trouble or cause you pain. I'm giving you the information you need to help your child.

I do not dislike your child. I'm not picking on him or being mean or saying he's weird. I'm just letting you know what I see. He's having problems. Many of my students have problems. I'm trying to help him, just like I try to help everyone else.

I recognize that your child is having a hard time, because I've been an educator for years and I know what to look for. I've taught hundreds of kids his age the same thing I'm trying to teach him now. I know how long it took them to learn it and how hard they

had to work. When I compare his progress to theirs, I can see he's struggling.

Over the years, I've watched the kids I've taught. I know how kids his age typically act. Not how they're "supposed" to act—how they do act. I know how they handle frustration and confusion and how they respond to boredom, Friday afternoons, rainy days, noisy assemblies, vacation time, and feuds among classmates. If I tell you your child's behavior is out of the ordinary, I know what I'm talking about.

Half the kids I've taught have been boys. I understand their behavior. I know they act differently and learn differently than girls; I've been teaching them successfully for years. Right now, your son is having trouble. The other boys in my class aren't. What I'm doing works for them, but your son isn't keeping up with the group. I didn't come to this conclusion because I don't understand boys. Your son is having a hard time.

When I tell you my concerns, I'm not blaming you. You can influence some of his behaviors, but not all of them. There are some skills you can teach him, and some you can't. Sometimes when I tell you these things, I'm asking for your help. I want you and I to work together to help him learn. Other times, I'm just keeping you informed.

If I say your child has difficulties, it doesn't mean I don't like him or that I'm giving up on him. I'm not throwing him away, I promise. I care enough about him to want to try to help.

It's not easy for me to tell you that your child is having a problem; no parent wants to hear that. It hurts, and it's scary, and sometimes it makes parents feel like failures. I don't enjoy doing that to you. And I don't like taking the risk that you're going to react badly. I've had parents yell at me, complain to my boss, or even physically attack me. I don't want to have to tell you that your child is struggling, but I will—because it's important. It's necessary, if your child is going to get the help he needs.

14

REALISM AND ACCEPTANCE

When I say you need to be realistic and accept your child's difficulties, I am not giving up on him. I'm not asking you to, either. I don't believe that your child today is "all he'll ever be." He's a living, growing person, with a whole life ahead of him, and I'm here to help him make the most of it. I'm not defining him by his diagnosis or saying he's limited by it. I'm not asking you to embrace his difficulties or say they're okay. When I ask you to be realistic and accept your child's difficulties, I'm asking you to look hard at the problems he has today and understand how they affect him.

That's it. You and I just have to be able to look at his difficulties. We don't have to like them, and we

don't have to use them to plan out his future. But, we have to accept that they're there and recognize them for what they are. If we don't, if we deny that he has problems or if we downplay them, then whatever we do won't address his needs. We'll miss out on our chance to help him.

If your car doesn't start, you don't refuse to believe it and sit in your driveway waiting for your car to magically arrive at the store. You also don't refuse to believe how much money you have in your bank account just because you'd rather have more. In both cases, bad things would happen if you didn't attend to the situation. You would never get to the store that way, and you might get yourself into a lot of financial trouble. There are a lot of things like that in life. There are some things we have to accept and deal with, whether we want to or not. Your child's difficulties are one of them.

The good news is that when it comes to cars and bank balances, you've got a chance to change the way they affect you. If your car is broken, you can try to fix it or replace it. If you know you're running low on money, you can work on ways to get more. If you know exactly what your difficulties are, you can take steps to try and resolve them. The same is true with your child.

To help your child, we need to first define his difficulties and figure out exactly what they are. Even if we don't want to look that close, and even if his problems scare us, we have to do it. There are problems that no parent wants to believe could ever affect his or her child, but sometimes they do, like it or not. When they occur, we have to decide what to do— believe the evidence and work to help the child? Or decide not to believe it because it's too hard to deal with and abandon the child to face it on his own?

Having a child with difficulties isn't easy. It's not easy for you or for me—but it's hardest on your child. The only way we can make it better for him is to face his problems head on. We have to look at his challenges realistically and accept that they are there. Once we know what they are, we can start looking for ways to make them better. He deserves that.

15
TEACHING INDEPENDENCE

Y ou want your child to be competent. You want him to be able to take care of himself and deal with the world and all its complexities the very best he can. You want him to become independent. I do, too.

Independence isn't something he can learn out of a book. It's something he has to practice. He has to recognize the value of doing things himself, have the confidence to try to work on his own, be proud of himself if he succeeds, and know what to do if he doesn't. Otherwise, he won't get anywhere. If he thinks he always needs help, he won't master anything. If he doesn't have the confidence or desire to try to learn new things, he won't. If he tries something and fails and doesn't know how to pick

himself up and start over again, he will quit trying at the first sign of trouble. The more independent your child is, the better he'll do in the long run. He'll learn more and have to rely less on other people. His chances of being able to create a happy life for himself increase significantly.

How do we teach independence? By having him do things for himself.

By expecting that your child will do things for himself as best he can, we build the idea in his head that he can and should try. If your backpack needs to get to school and your parent carries it for you every day, you will never learn to carry it because you won't have to. But if you are told it's your job to do it, that you're quite capable of doing it, that no one else is going to do it, and that there will be consequences if you don't, you'll learn. This teaches a child responsibility, competency, and independence.

And, if one day your backpack is too heavy for you to carry, you learn to problem solve. Either you have to ask for help and make a good case for why you need it, or you have to figure out another solution for getting your backpack to school. If you come up with a way to get it there, you can be proud that you solved the problem, and you'll be a bit more confident that you can solve the next one that comes along.

That's why, unless your child has physical difficulties that make him absolutely incapable of carrying his backpack, we're going to make him responsible for it. And we're going to look at you funny if you do it for him. If his backpack is too heavy, we're going to let him figure out how to solve that problem. If he needs help, we're going to give it to him, but not until we're sure he needs it. And, we're only going to give him as much help as he needs. That way, he learns how to get his backpack to school himself. This process works—unless you derail it. Even if you have the best of intentions, if you step in and do something for him when he is capable of doing it for himself, then either he'll learn that he is incompetent, or he'll learn to manipulate you to do his work for him. And these are the only things he will learn.

Of course, carrying his backpack is only one of the many skills he's going to need to make it in the world. We want him to learn as much as possible. So, we're going to push him to do as much as he can, as often as he can—from learning to buy his lunch, to doing his homework, to talking to his guidance counselor himself. We want him to learn the skills, but we also want him to be able to figure out what he needs to learn and how to do it. Once your child gets out of high school, having those skills is important. Without them, it's pretty tough to hold a job or learn to navigate a college campus.

Some students have aides who help them in the classroom. Aides are a mixed blessing. Their job is to enable a child to participate in a classroom environment that he couldn't be a part of otherwise. They also try to teach him how to function in that classroom without their help. A good aide tries to put herself out of a job. She wants to help your child work as independently as possible. If she doesn't actively try to teach him independence, then she's teaching him to be dependent.

As your child gets older, we're going to push him to do more for himself. Always. Every time he graduates to the next grade, he's going to be expected to become more independent. Sixth-grade teachers are not as warm and fuzzy as first-grade teachers. That's because it's bad for sixth graders to be treated like first graders, even if they have special needs. Kids with special needs may need more help than other sixth-grade students, but we want to make sure they need a lot less than they did when they were in first grade. Part of expecting your child to do more for himself is expecting you to do less for him. So each year, when your child's new teacher seems to be telling you to butt out a little more than last year's teacher did, it's not because she doesn't want you to be involved. It's because she wants you to be involved at the level your child needs this year, not at the level he needed last year. Sometimes part of our job is to peel parents off their kids. Not completely—just enough so their children can grow.

We are going to keep teaching your child to become more competent. We're going to push him into new situations. We have to push him far enough that he's learning, but not so far that he falls flat on his face. We're not always going to know how far that is. Sometimes he's going to fail. It's guaranteed; that's part of learning new skills. When he does fail, we'll help him deal with it. Either we'll help him learn the skills he needs to succeed, or we'll decide he's not ready to learn that particular skill set yet. We'll pull him back until he's ready to try again. Failure is part of life, and we need to teach him to deal with that, too.

Teaching your child independence is really important, and we take it seriously. Sometimes the way we do it might look like we don't want to help him. That's not true. We are helping him. We're teaching him how to help himself.

16

SPECIAL EDUCATION IS CHANGING

Our view of special education is changing. Special education used to mean being assigned to a particular classroom, one typically located far away from the rest of the classrooms, where the kids who "weren't that bright" went to learn. They were considered nice kids, but not smart enough to keep up with the rest of the students, and they certainly didn't belong in the same classroom as everybody else. They were—you know—*different*.

We don't think that way anymore. Kids in special education are just as much a part of our school and school life as all the other kids are. They've got the same rights and privileges and, barring severe behavioral problems, can attend the same classes as the rest of our students.

Our goal is to place children in the classes where they can learn what they need to learn—to present lessons at the level the students need and in a way they can access them. If a child needs remedial math, we want him in the room that teaches remedial math. If he struggles with reading but is otherwise able to take honors science, then we want him in honors science, with support that will help him overcome his reading difficulties. If he can do general-education work but demonstrates really odd behaviors and blurts out in the classroom, we want to support him, his classmates, and his teacher so he can stay in the general-education classroom as much as possible. Receiving special education doesn't mean being sent to that far-off classroom anymore. Special education means giving a child the help he needs.

It used to be that if your child was placed in a special-education classroom, he would probably be in one for the rest of his time in school. The thinking was, "once in special education, *always* in special education." Now, our goal is to incorporate as many kids as we can into the general-education setting.

Kids need to be taught at the level at which they can learn, in a way they can learn it. We work to remove as many of the barriers as possible that keep students from being a part of the general-education environment. We want them to learn at the highest level they can, and we want them to be able to interact with their typically developing peers. Once your child gets out of high school, he's going to go out into the real world, where others may not understand his difficulties. They will expect him to have the same abilities that they do and for him to act the same as everyone else. We want to make him as capable and independent as possible, so he can succeed out there.

Years ago, you were either a special-education student or a general-education student. Now you can be both. If some of your child's needs are best met in a special-education classroom, we'll want him to spend time there. If some of them are best met in a general-education classroom, then we'll want him there, too. Your child can be in one room or the other or both; we can divide his day so he gets the learning opportunities he needs in the way he needs them. If he has a low level of academic skills but he's able to interact with typically developing kids, then we'll want him in special education for academic classes and in general education for music, art, and PE. If he's doing well academically but needs help socially, then perhaps he can be placed in general education with pull-out classes to work on social skills. We've got a lot of options these days, and we use them.

It used to be that few general-education teachers knew how to teach kids with disabilities. Most of us still don't, but we're starting to learn. We're learning that kids with special needs belong in general education, too. We're figuring out why our students do what they do and how to help them. We're looking into new tools to help our kids overcome their difficulties or work around them. And, we're learning that, while teaching children with special needs can be difficult, it can be very rewarding, too.

Today, we've got a lot of options in special education. Having your child in special education doesn't mean he gets sent away from the regular classroom and forgotten. It means he's got a lot of people with a lot of resources working to help him learn. Our goal is to make your child as capable of functioning in the general-education world as much as possible, so that when he graduates into the real world, he can succeed there too. Special education isn't a destination. It's a way-stop on his educational journey.

17

LIVING, VOCATIONAL, AND SOCIAL SKILLS

If we teach your child the math necessary to make change in a monetary transaction but don't teach him politeness, he won't be able to work with the public, even if he can run a cash register.

If we teach him engineering skills, but he keeps losing his temper, he won't stay employed, no matter how smart he is.

If he doesn't know how to bathe and keep his clothes clean, no one will hire him.

If he doesn't know where to go for help when he needs it on a college campus, he may wind up dropping out of school.

If he doesn't know how to cook, pay bills, clean house, or grocery shop, he won't be able to live independently.

If he doesn't know how to behave in romantic situations, he may get arrested or put himself in danger.

If he doesn't know how to get around town safely, he might get hurt, and he may not be able to get a job or go to school.

If he has an aide all throughout school and never learns independence, he will be unemployable.

If he cannot connect with people, he'll live in isolation, and his risk of developing depression and committing suicide will be higher.

Academics are important, but the other skills your child needs to make it through life are just as important. If he does poorly academically but has good coping skills, he can still have a good life. But if his coping skills are bad, he'll never be able to succeed in life. If he doesn't learn to solve problems and think for himself, it won't matter how many times he's hired, because his job won't last. Few employers will keep an employee who needs constant direction and attention. If he's headed to college, it won't matter which universities accept him, because college life will be overwhelming, and he won't finish his coursework. It's not enough that we teach our kids how to get good grades in school. We have to teach them what they need to be able to make a life for themselves after they get out of high school.

Fortunately, as educators, we're starting to focus more on giving your child opportunities to learn those skills. The vocational, social, and life skills curriculums in our special-education classes are getting more attention. As our expectations for what students with special needs can do have increased, we've started to re-examine what we're teaching them and why. We're looking more at the needs of the whole child, not just the academic needs demonstrated on tests required by the state.

So if your child has special needs, at some point, we may suggest shifting some of our emphasis from academic goals to working on vocational and life skills goals. For instance, if he's in high school, we may decide it's a good idea to pull him out of one of his college-oriented classes and instead put him in a work transition class.

This idea upsets a lot of parents. They think the reason we want to transfer their child out of some of his academic classes and put him to work in the cafeteria is that we're giving up on him. They think we're saying, "He's a special-education kid. He's not smart enough to go to college." But we're not. We're focusing on giving him the tools he needs so he can make it in life after high school. He needs to learn how to get along with teammates, problem solve, and ask for help when he needs it. In work transition classes, he is placed in a structured environment, where we can set up lessons in coping skills, time management, and emotional control. By shifting his focus to include vocational, social, and life skills, we're not interfering with his academic education. We're giving him the skills he needs so he can continue it when he no longer has our help.

Today, your child's life skills may not seem that important to you. Right now, when he needs help, you can take care of things. You can smooth out life's troubles, or at least help him navigate them. You're there to step in whenever he needs it. Even if he doesn't know he needs help, you're there. You can provide transportation so he can get to work and buy groceries when his cupboards are bare. If he can't get a job or live alone, that's okay, because he can stay with you. Maybe you think it's better if he lives at home anyway, because then you won't have to worry, and it will be easier for you to take care of him. A lot of parents think that way.

But one day, you're not going to be there. What happens then?

We know your child's academic skills are important. Wherever he falls on the academic scale, whether it's in remedial, general, or honors classes, your child's core education is important to us, too. Having a good foundation in math, language, literature, history, and science will have a huge impact on his future, whether he pursues a higher education, transitions straight into the working world, or follows a different path. Having a good academic foundation is critical for your child to be able to find success in life, but it's not the only factor. His life skills, vocational skills, and social skills are just as important, and we need to give them our attention, too. Please let us.

18

THE FUTURE

I don't know what the future holds for your child. I wish I did.

For instance, I don't know who your child's teacher will be next year. I may have an idea, but sometimes teachers retire, are reassigned, or move away. The number of students attending our school changes, and so do our budgets. Sometimes we know what's going to happen before school ends for the summer, and sometimes we don't. I'm not even positive I'll be at this school next year. So I can't guarantee that your child will be assigned to a particular teacher. I will, however, do my best to make sure that next year's teacher is a good match for your child.

Since I don't know the future, sometimes I may not pick out the best program for your child right

away. I may think he'll succeed in one type of classroom or with one type of support and then find out later I was wrong. I may believe he's ready for an environment that requires more independence and capabilities than he currently has, or I may think he's not ready, when he really is. But that's okay, because we can make changes. If things aren't going well, you and I can try to come up with something that works better. If you have concerns, come see me, and we'll figure out what to do. Just because it isn't working right now doesn't mean I don't care or won't work to fix it.

I also don't know what kind of progress your child will make this year. I can tell you what progress I'd like him to make, and I can tell you what we'll be working on. But, I don't know how fast he'll learn. He may take off like a rocket, or he may learn a little slower. That's okay. I'll be ready for him, whatever his pace. When he meets his goals, you and I will come up with new ones. I won't quit teaching him just because he's learning faster than we expected. And, if he isn't reaching his goals, we can look at them again and decide if they're the right ones or if we need to change our methods. Whatever your child's learning pace, I'll keep him challenged and moving forward.

If your child is in a special-education classroom, I can't tell you when he'll be ready to start attending a general-education class. I know we're working toward it. I can tell you which skills he needs to learn before we send him into general education, and I can tell you what our plan is to get him there. But whether it will be this year or next, I really can't say.

I don't know what your child will be capable of by the time he leaves school. I'd like to be able to tell you if he'll make it to college or if he'll be able to hold a job or if he'll be living with you for the rest of his life. It would make it easier for you and me. But, I don't know for sure what his capabilities will be. I know where he is now, and I know what he needs to learn next, so I focus my attention there, teaching him step by step so he can make it as far as he can go. That's all I can do, but that's okay, because it's what he needs right now.

I don't have a crystal ball. I wish I did. All our lives would be easier if I always knew what was going to happen. But just because I can't predict your child's future doesn't mean I don't have a plan, that I'm clueless, or that I don't care. It means that my plan is flexible, and that as new information comes up, you and I will refine it. We'll tailor it as we go along, fitting it to his needs as they change. We may not be able to set your child's path in stone from the beginning, but that's okay. We have the tools to shape his path as we discover where he's going.

19

IF YOU HAVE QUESTIONS, ASK ME

You and I are part of a team. If you have questions, ask me.

As in any workplace, school personnel use a lot of jargon. We use technical terms, abbreviations, slang, governmental policy names and numbers, and the names of various assessments and programs. Sometimes when we talk to you, we forget that you don't know all that we know. We're not trying to confuse you or be rude—honestly. We're just using the language of our workplace. If I went to where you work, I would probably hear you use terminology I don't understand. The same happens when you come into my realm at school. I'll try to remember to explain things to you as we go along, but since some parents are new to our world and

some are old hands, I'm really not sure what you know and what you don't. So, if you don't understand something I say, please stop me and ask me to explain. I won't mind, and I won't think you're stupid. I'll think you're a parent who's really trying hard to do the best for your child.

If you don't know the purpose of a meeting we're having and what we hope to accomplish, stop the meeting and ask. It's important that you know what our goals are and what we're trying to decide. I've attended IEP meetings and learned later that the parents didn't know why they were there, and I've been in discipline meetings and discovered the parents didn't know the possible outcomes being considered. I wasn't aware the parents were confused; otherwise, I would have explained to them what was happening. I didn't find out until afterward that they didn't know. We had sent them our standard meeting notification letter, and we weren't aware that they didn't understand what we meant. When you come to a meeting, make sure you know why we're meeting, what we're trying to decide, and what the results may be.

If you're unclear about the assessments we've done, what they measure, or what the results mean, ask. Assessments are tests that tell us what your child's needs and strengths are. It's important that you understand them. If we have very different views about your child's needs and capabilities, we're going to have a hard time agreeing on the best way to teach him.

Assessment scores can be difficult to figure out, especially since there are a lot of different ways to score them. Sometimes they are used to measure your child's abilities in terms of age or grade level. For example, we may find that although he's in the sixth grade, he is reading at a ninth-grade level. Some assessments serve to rate his scores against a national average. Others may have a scoring system based on a percentage of 100%, or a scale of 1 to 10, or 1 to 50, or 1 to 142. Also, some of the assessments relate to others; for instance, a score may be calculated on the basis of some combination of subtest scores. When we report the assessment results to you, we'll do our best to explain what they mean, but if you still have questions, let us know. Please, tell us if you're feeling lost or confused. We will be happy to explain. You're part of this team, and it's important that you have all the information we do.

Sometimes when we list choices for your child's classroom placement, programs, or instructional methods, we may not tell you all the options. That's not because we're trying to keep them from you. It's because we're not telling you about the ones we feel are inappropriate. If there's an autism program on the other side of the district, but it's for students who function at a lower level than your child does, we're probably not going to bring it up. If a class has a teacher we don't believe would be a good match for your child, we may not include her class on the list of options. If we don't think your child needs a particular service (on the basis of his assessment scores), we're not going to talk about options for giving him that service, and if we think we've got a great program that will meet his needs, we may not tell you about other programs. We may have good reasons for not listing all the options, but this can make parents feel like they were forced into accepting whatever we felt like offering. So, you can ask us to tell you all the options, even the ones we don't think are good selections. That way, you'll understand why we offered the ones we did.

If you don't know why we made a particular decision, ask. We're not trying to keep information from you. There are reasons behind our choices, and if I forget to tell them to you, just ask. Sometimes we don't have as much control over our decisions as we'd like—we may be choosing from existing programs or following state laws, but you should understand how and why our decisions were made. You're part of the decision-making process, too. You may not always agree with us, but if we disagree, it shouldn't be because we don't understand each other.

If something happens that you don't understand, ask. But please—ask nicely. Make an appointment to meet with me, so I can devote my full attention to you; don't stop me in the hall when I'm late for class and demand an immediate conference. Keep your tone polite, and don't be demanding or insulting. Don't assume I'm being secretive and trying to trick you. Give me the benefit of the doubt and let me explain. If you don't understand my explanation, let me know, and I'll explain some more. Ask me before you ask my supervisor. If you've talked to me a few times but we're not getting anywhere, then please go ask my boss, and maybe she can help us out.

You're working hard to help your child. I am, too. We may not always agree on the best way to do that, but our disagreements shouldn't result from misunderstandings. If you're ever unsure about what's going on, ask me. The more information you have, the better we can both help your child.

20

HOMEWORK

T here is no way I can possibly teach your child everything he needs to learn by myself. I need your help.

Your child has a tremendous amount of information he needs to absorb—more than other kids his age. Not only does he need to learn the academics they do, but he also needs to learn the social interaction and life skills other kids pick up naturally. It's a lot for him to learn and a lot for me to teach.

He can't do it all on his own—if he could, he wouldn't have a disability. If I could teach him everything myself, I would, but I can't. Autism isn't that easy. Some parents say it's not their job to educate their children—they believe it's my job alone, because it's what I get paid for. They're right, I do get paid

to teach children. But, if I'm doing everything I can to help your child and he's still struggling, then you have a choice to make. You can ignore the situation, you can blame me, or you can do what you can to help him, too.

One day not long from now, your child will leave my class. If he's having a hard time after he leaves, I'll be sad. I'll feel bad that he's having difficulties. Then, in a few months or years, my memories of him will fade. He'll be out of my life, and I'll be focused on helping other students. But, your child will still be in your life. Whether or not he learns the most he can while he's at school will affect your family for a very long time. Isn't it worth it to put in the time and effort now, so he can get all he can out of school? Help me to help him. The sooner his skills improve, the easier his life will be.

I know you do a lot already. It's not easy raising a child with special needs. You have other family members to care for, a household to run, and possibly a job. Your child with autism may need outside therapies and more doctor appointments than other children do. You likely experience more stress than most other parents, and your financial burden is probably bigger. And, somewhere in all that, your family needs to just enjoy being a family, too.

I know you can't do everything, and I'm not asking you to. Just do the best you can. We can do a lot more by working together than we can by struggling alone.

A big way you can help is to make sure your child does his homework. That's not always easy, I know—but it's important. Doing homework gives him a chance to practice what he learns in school. If he's having a hard time with a particular subject, doing homework will help him. Just like practice is important when someone is learning to play a sport or a musical instrument, it helps when a child is learning to read, too—or write, do math, or learn history or any other subject. That's why I assign homework. It's not because I really like spending my evening grading papers; it's because the more time a student spends practicing a skill, the better he gets.

I know that doing homework with children with special needs can be tough. Really tough. There can be screaming, yelling, and tears—by kids and parents. It can be tempting to give up. Don't. If you're having a hard time getting homework done, come talk to me. Sometimes, if we work together, we can come up with ideas that will make homework time easier.

For instance, most children with autism do better when tasks are structured. Then they know what's expected of them and what they need to get done before they can go do what they really want to do. Structuring homework time makes it easier for your child. Have a place for him to do his homework that doesn't have a lot of distractions. If noise bothers him, find a quiet spot. If he gets distracted by having toys around, have him do his homework in a toy-free zone, like the kitchen. Make sure the supplies he needs are handy. Help him manage his time, too. Come up with a routine that works for your family. It doesn't have to be rigid—things will happen occasionally, like doctor's appointments and family events. But keep it as consistent as you can, so he'll learn that homework is just part of life, whether he likes it or not. And, if he takes medication, try to get homework done before his medication wears off for the day.

Your child may need to work someplace where you can supervise him. You might need to stay in the same room or sit at the table with him. Sometimes parents say, "I shouldn't have to do that." That may be true, but in the world of special education, there is no "should"—there is only "what is." If it helps, do it. He won't always need you there, but he does now. Put the time in now, so he can learn the skills he needs and become less dependent on you later. All the struggles you help him through today really will make him more capable as he gets older.

If your child is having a hard time doing his homework, it may be because he doesn't know what he's supposed to do. He might not have heard the assignment, or he may have misunderstood the directions. If he participates in pull-out services during the school day, he might have been out of the classroom when the homework was assigned. Or, he may not understand how to do the work. If you can help him figure it out, great. If not, tell him to ask me to explain it to him. That way, he learns to ask for help when he needs it, which is not always an easy task for people with autism. If that doesn't work, contact me yourself. E-mail me, leave a message at the school, or write me a note for your child to give me. We can arrange a time for him, or both of you, to come in, and I'll explain how to do the work.

Sometimes, I can make accommodations for him or modify his homework. I can't always do this, but you can ask. *Accommodations* are things we can do to help him complete his assignments, like letting him type the answers to his worksheet on a separate piece of paper if writing is difficult for him. *Modifications* are when I change the homework he's expected to turn in—for instance, I can cut down the number of problems he has to do or give him extra time. Implementing accommodations and modifications can make it easier for your child to get his homework done.

But, be careful if you change what you expect your child to do for homework. Make sure we're not changing it so much that he loses out on learning. If writing is hard for him, but we're still working to improve his writing skills, making it so he never has write isn't going to help him. He still needs the practice. We don't want his writing difficulties to affect what he's learning in class, but at the same time, we need to make sure he still writes.

Some kids just refuse to do homework. It's not uncommon to hear a child with autism say that schoolwork is supposed to be done at school, not at home, and not over the weekend. They're against it on principle. Or, they may just not want to do it. They may also refuse to do the work because they already know how to do it, so they don't see why they should have to do it again.

I can't solve this problem for you. It's entirely out of my arena. Getting kids with special needs to do homework when they don't want to is a hard part of a parent's job. But, I can tell you that it's important for you to make your child do his homework. Not for me or for his grades or so school personnel will "like him better." He has to do it because he has to know that sometimes he has to do things he doesn't want to do—even if he thinks they're stupid. When he gets to college, they're not going to care if he wants to do his homework or not. If it's required and he doesn't do it, he'll flunk out of college. Period. Even if he has a disability. When he gets a job, he's going to have to do what the boss tells him, whether he likes it or not. Even if he thinks it's pointless. Otherwise, he'll get fired from every job he ever gets. When a police officer tells him to do something, if your child argues, the consequences can be even worse. Do your child a favor and make him do his homework, whether he wants to or not.

Homework time can be hard for all students—especially those with special needs. But, it's important. Doing homework now will make your child's life easier when he's an adult. If you need help with homework, ask and I'll see if I can help. But don't give up. The work you put in now is an investment in your child's future.

21

CONSULTATIONS

The educators at your child's school have a lot of combined knowledge about how to teach children. Take advantage of it. If you're working with your child at home to improve his skills and you hit a roadblock, ask us for advice.

One of the areas parents of children with special needs sometimes have questions about is childhood development. They want to know what typical behavior looks like for kids their child's age. Or, to put it another way, how far from typical development is their child in a particular area? Do most kids know how to read by the time they're 6 years old? How many are still struggling at the age of 7 or 8? Kindergarten boys still hit each other occasionally, but how unusual is it for a second-grade boy to hit one

of his classmates? What about a fourth-grader? How many kids need tutoring occasionally? At what age do girls start to get boy crazy? How many of them get really boy crazy? How many kids know what they want to do after high school by the time they're 16? How many 18-year-olds have realistic plans for how to accomplish their goals?

General-education teachers know a lot about childhood development. We work with it every day. Someone who has taught third grade for several years has observed hundreds of third-graders. She's a great resource if you've got questions about 8- and 9-year-olds. She's seen most of the problems third-graders face and has helped counsel them and their families through all kinds of troubles. If you've got questions, ask her. She can't talk to you about particular students, but she can give you a lot of insight into the behavior of students in third grade.

Teachers also sometimes switch grade levels. That third-grade teacher may also have taught fifth grade or middle school. She may be able to tell you what's typical for kids in the grades ahead of you. That's handy when you're trying to get your child ready for next year. She can tell you which behaviors kids and teachers in that grade find acceptable and which they don't. For instance, by sixth grade, kids don't play tag so much, trading cards are out, and school personnel really start to disapprove of students hugging each other at school. If you know some of the behaviors your child needs to change before he gets to a higher grade, you can start working on changing them now. It will make his transition a lot easier.

If your child is having a hard time in a particular subject, ask his teacher how you can help him at home. Over the years, she's probably seen and tried a lot of different teaching methods. If the strategies she's currently using in the classroom aren't working for your child, maybe one of the others she knows will. If you need more ideas, try asking the teachers who work with struggling students. Schools have different names for these classes—*the resource room, the learning lab,* or *after-school tutoring,* to name a few. Teachers who primarily work with kids who have difficulties have a lot of experience in nurturing their skills. Your child may not officially qualify for time in those teachers' classes, but often if you ask to meet with them after school, they'll be delighted to give you ideas that might help at home.

Not all children with special needs are in special-education classrooms. But even if your child isn't, your school's special-education teachers may still be willing to give you some advice. It wouldn't hurt to stop by after school someday and see if they wouldn't mind sharing some ideas. After all, they're experts at figuring out how to help kids with special needs grasp new ideas.

If your child receives specialized services from the school, like adaptive PE or speech or occupational therapy, consider asking his therapist or teacher for ideas. For example, if your child needs to develop his finger strength to be able to write more easily, his occupational therapist may be willing to give you exercises you can do at home. Few parents think to ask for homework from these types of teachers, yet their children's skills will improve much faster if they work on them at home in addition to doing the therapy the child receives at school.

Of course, unless a teacher has your child as a student, she doesn't have to help you. Most teachers really like working with children and are happy to see a struggling child overcome his difficulties. Many of them will be glad to give you a few ideas. But be respectful of the fact that a teacher is taking time away from her work or using her free time to help you. Don't abuse her kindness by demanding too much of her time or by expecting her to tutor your child. The idea is that you're asking for her advice. That said, it's rare for a teacher to turn down a parent who is really working hard to help his or her child.

Working with your child at home isn't always easy. Helping him overcome his difficulties may mean doing research, buying supplies, and spending a lot of time at the homework table. It may require a lot of effort from both you and your child. But, it's worth it. Every small improvement your child makes in developing his skills means his life will be a little easier. Each step moves him a little farther forward on his journey. You may not be able to ease his difficulties entirely, but every little bit of improvement helps.

The combined knowledge of the professionals at your child's school is a fantastic resource. Use it.

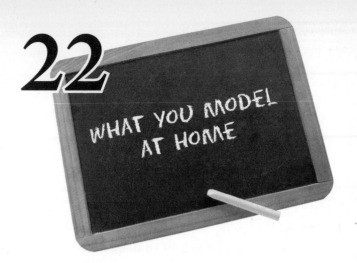

22

WHAT YOU MODEL AT HOME

Your child is in my care for about 6 hours a day. He's in your care for the other 18. Even after you subtract the time he spends sleeping, he's around you far more than he's around me. You have more influence over him than I do, and that's good. He's your child, and that's what parenting is all about. But if I'm teaching him one behavior at school and you're teaching him another at home, we're not going to get very far.

I know you can't control every bit of your child's behavior and attitude. If you could, you would. Your child wouldn't have special needs, and we wouldn't need parent-teacher conferences. Homework and chores would always get done. Your child would never yell at a classmate, a teacher, or you.

Temper tantrums would be a thing of the past, and you'd never again have to apologize for something rude your child has said or done. If you could immediately stop his inappropriate behavior, you would. I understand that autism affects what he says and how he acts. But you do, too.

Parenting isn't easy. Sometimes it demands more strength, courage, and wisdom than any human has. Nobody is perfect. I don't expect you to be, either. Even the best parents pass a few unhelpful habits or attitudes on to their child, along with all the good they give him. They don't mean to, and they usually don't know they're teaching their child things that will make his life more difficult. But they are. And it's difficult, if not impossible, for me to teach him something different than what he's living at home.

For example, your child hears what you say at home, and then he repeats it at school. That doesn't mean if he says something rude or bad at school he must have learned it at home. There are a lot of places he could have picked it up, and home is just one of them. It also doesn't mean that you approve of everything he says. I know you don't, and I know you've tried to correct him. What I'm saying is that some of the things you say at home get repeated at school. If you swear at home, your child will swear at school. And he'll get in trouble for it. If you make comments about other people's race, religion, gender, or sexual orientation, your child will repeat your words at school. Your beliefs are your business, and you have every right to have them. But if your child doesn't know when it's okay to voice controversial opinions and when it's not, he's going to have a hard time getting along with other students. In fact, it will probably make him a prime target for bullies. Your child's social difficulties mean he can't always tell when it's better to express his opinions or keep them to himself.

If you talk poorly about me and other teachers in front of your child at home, I'll never be able to get his respect at school. He won't listen to me, because he'll have learned from you that what I think isn't important, that I'm dumb, or that I don't care about him. If I don't have his respect, I can't teach him. It's that simple.

If you don't have your child learn to do things on his own, he'll think he can't work independently. You'll teach him that someone has to help him or do things for him. Always. Even if it's something he could learn how to do himself, he'll sit and wait until someone comes along to help. That's not good. It means he'll never learn how to solve problems or have confidence in his abilities. It means he won't master new skills. He won't be able to advance academically or learn how to take care of himself, and when he gets older, he won't be able to keep a job. He has to learn that he can do things himself— without Mom, a teacher, an aide, or a sibling doing things for him. When he's an adult, you'll want him to be as independent as possible. No employer is going to want his mother to come to work with him.

If you don't make sure your child does his homework and chores, you will teach him that if he doesn't feel like doing something, he doesn't have to, and that someone else will do his job for him. Or, he'll think it doesn't matter if he ignores assignments—eventually they'll just go away. If you teach him when he's a child that he doesn't have to do his homework, even though his teacher tells him to, how is he going to act when he grows up and his boss tells him to do something? Or a policeman? Or a judge? Or a doctor? Not to mention, how will he develop the skills the homework and chores are supposed to teach him in the first place?

Does your child's disability mean he's not as capable as other kids his age? Yes. Does it mean he's incapable? No. Not unless you teach him that he is. Is autism an excuse for him to not learn how to behave politely? No. It means it's more difficult for him to learn how to behave politely. Will he master all the details of social interaction? Probably not. But if he doesn't feel that he's capable of learning how to get along with people, or if he believes that having a disability means he doesn't have to learn, then he's not going to learn anything. If you teach him that having autism is an excuse to not try to improve his skills, his life will be harder than it has to be. So will yours.

One of my students with autism would occasionally hit other students. His mom told the parents of those children, "He has autism. That's what children with autism do." At first the other parents were sympathetic, but as the school year went on, they understandably got more upset—with the child, with me, and with his mom. They were mad at the child for hitting their kids, with me for not preventing it from happening, and with the mom, who only ever said, "That's what children with autism do." She used autism as an excuse for his behavior. He did, too. If you asked him why he hit the other kids, he'd say, "Because I have autism." Eventually, we had to move him out of my class to protect the other children.

Nobody is perfect. Not you, and not me. Even if you were the most perfect parent and never demonstrated bad behavior in front of your child, he would still have some behavioral difficulties. I know you are not causing his autism or the things he does at school that create so much trouble for him. But, you do have some influence over his attitudes and behavior. Please use whatever influence you have to help him build his skills and make his life easier.

23

FUNDING

By law, we need to provide your child with a free and appropriate education that prepares him for further education, employment, and independent living. Federal law also defines some of the services we may need to provide to meet your child's needs.

Our school district is required to give your child specialized services if he needs them, but the federal government only pays for a portion of those services. It costs our district more money to educate your child than to educate a typically developing child. The federal and state governments give us only part of the money needed to cover that additional expense. We have to take the rest of the money from our general budget—the money that

we use to educate all of our students. Each addition-al service we give your child costs us money. The more we spend on your child, the less we have to spend on other children—both typically developing students and those in special education.

That's a cold, hard fact. Every dollar we spend on special-education services has to come from some-where. Some of it comes from the federal and state governments, but the rest comes out of our district's pocket. We can't make money grow on trees any more than you can. We have budgets. If we run out of money, we run out. Just like you. If we spend more in one area of our budget, we have to spend less in another.

We have to spend more money to educate your child than we do other children. But we're okay with that. Really. We know your child has more needs than other students, and we know his edu-cation will cost more. That's just part of teaching kids with special needs. Just like we have to bud-get a certain amount of money to buy classroom supplies and library books, we have to budget money to pay for special education. It's part of life. We don't mind it, and it's worth it to us so we can help your child become competent, independent, and productive.

State and federal law says we have to meet your child's educational needs and pay for the services to do so, and that's where the debate between parents and school districts really heats up. What exactly are the educational needs of each child, and what are the best ways to meet those needs? When good parents, good teachers, and good administrators all care about a student but have different ideas about how to help him, sometimes it triggers a battle.

There are admittedly a few schools in which decisions are made about services provided to children on the basis of cost. Those schools exist, and this practice is deplorable, but it's rare. Most school personnel work hard to figure out how to stretch their budget dollars to provide the best help for the most students we can. We don't mind using some of our budget to provide services to children who need them, but we want to make sure we're not wasting the money we spend.

One of the ways schools work to provide services is to run remedial programs in-house. For instance, instead of sending 10 students to a math tutoring program in the next city over, we might train one of our teachers to run the same or a different math program after school, on our campus. That way, we can still give those 10 children quality tutoring in math, but we can do it at a lower cost and also make it available to more students. The less money we spend sending a few students outside our district, the more we can spend on educating all the students inside our district.

Sometimes, a parent will decide they don't want to use our in-school services. They've found another program they like better, and they'd like us to pay for it. That's okay, if our in-house tutoring programs don't work for your child. But please make sure they don't work before you ask us to pay for something else. Try our school's programs first. If your child isn't making progress in our programs, then we can talk about other options. But don't ask us to spend extra money unless we've proven that what we currently have doesn't work for your child.

Also, don't ask us to spend dollars defending against lawsuits or due process hearings over problems we could have solved without legal help. If you're unhappy about something, make sure you've talked to everyone in our school and district who may be able to help, before you involve the courts. Don't yell at us—talk with us. Make an appointment, and let's see if we can come up with a workable solution. If you've examined all your options and really feel that the only way to get what your child needs is to file suit against us, then go ahead.

Fight for your child. But if you haven't tried everything else first, please reconsider. Lawsuits not only damage your working relationship with the staff at our school; they're also very expensive. They require money to be used from the special-education budget that could be used to provide much-needed services for kids.

If your child doesn't need a service, please don't ask us to provide it. If he really doesn't need an aide or if he's grown to the point that an aide is getting in the way of him learning independence, then don't ask for one. If he doesn't need special-education transportation or tutoring or occupational therapy, don't insist on him having it. We want to provide the services he really needs, but it doesn't make sense to waste money on things he doesn't.

Again, by law, our school district is required to provide your child with a free and appropriate education that prepares him for further education, employment, and independent living. Our funding difficulties cannot prevent us from meeting your child's educational needs. It's okay to make sure that we spend the money necessary to educate your child. But please don't ask us to spend money if it's not necessary. Every dollar we waste is one we could have spent helping a child.

24

MEDICATING YOUR CHILD

It is illegal for any school official to tell parents they must give their child a controlled substance for him to be able to attend school. This includes medications to treat ADHD and other conditions. It's illegal. Period. Federal law doesn't allow wiggle room.

School districts enforce this rule. Teachers are not allowed to insist that their students take medication. So why am I even bringing this up?

Because I care about your child.

First, let's be clear. If I'm suggesting that you talk to your doctor about medicating your child, I'm not representing the school. I'm speaking for myself. There is no way the school is going to risk going against the federal government on this. And, if I talk

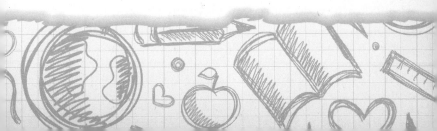

to you about this issue, I'm not demanding or insist-
ing anything. I'm suggesting. I'm giving you advice.
You're looking for ways to help your child, and I'm
sharing my ideas with you. That's all. If you're not
interested in taking my advice, that's fine. Just say,
"Thanks, but no thanks."

You're the parent. It's your choice whether or
not to medicate your child—not mine. My job is to
educate the children who are placed in my class—all
of them, in whatever state they arrive. I'll devote the
same amount of time and energy to teaching your
child, no matter what medical decisions you make.
Whether or not you give your child medicine is a
decision that is between you and your child's doctor.
I've got no place in that equation. I'm not a medical
professional, and I cannot give medical advice. I'm
not trying to.

I'm giving you my personal advice, as someone
who has spent years in the classroom, observing children as they learn. I know the problems they face, and
I've watched as they and their families have worked to
overcome them. For some of my students, medication
has been part of their family's solution. If I talk to
you about considering medication for your child, I'm
simply sharing my observations about what I've seen
medications do for some kids in my classroom.

Has medication worked for every child? No. In some cases, their parents tried it and found it to be ineffective, or they didn't like the side effects. But, it has worked for many of my students. I've seen medication change the lives of some of my kids. It's increased their attention span and decreased the incidence of behaviors that got them into trouble. It's reduced their anxiety, and it's improved their ability to get along in the classroom and on the playground. Their self-esteem has grown, their grades have improved, and they've developed the ability to make and keep friends. Granted, medication by itself was not the only factor in their success. Behavioral therapy played an important part, too. But behavioral therapy by itself wasn't working for these students. When the children started taking medication, the behavioral therapy began to work better.

I know that if I suggest medication to you, I'm taking a risk. You could go to my principal and complain. But please, take my words as they are meant, as advice from one person who cares about your child to another. I know you're looking for ideas to help him. If I've got information I think could make a difference, I want to give it to you, even if it means I'm taking a chance. That's how much I care about your child.

25

GET TO KNOW US

It can be hard to trust strangers to take care of your child. Unless you know us, it's easy to think of us as part of a bureaucracy that's more concerned with budgets than children. You don't know who we are, why we do what we do, or if we even know what we're doing. If all you see of us is brief encounters at meetings when we talk about your child's difficulties and what services to give him, it can be hard to trust us.

So come to the school and get to know us.

The best way for you to learn about us is to volunteer. Come to the school and roll up your sleeves. As we work together, you'll learn a lot. You'll get to meet the teachers and administrators and see us in action. You'll see how we react to the challenges we

face, what our priorities are, and how we treat our students. By getting to know how our classrooms operate, you'll be able to make better decisions about how we can all support your child best. You'll have more information when it comes to making placement decisions for next year, and if you know the teachers already, you won't spend your summer worrying about the start of the school year. Getting to know us will relieve a lot of your uncertainty about your child's education.

If you volunteer at your child's school, you'll also learn more about him and the way he interacts with others. As you watch him on campus, you'll be able to see firsthand how he reacts to his peers, school staff, and challenges in the classroom. By observing other students, you'll get a better idea of your child's strengths and difficulties. Spending time on campus will also give you a better feel for the demands placed on your child each day and whether they're appropriate. There's no substitute for the information you can get by putting in a little time at our school.

Also, the more time you spend on campus, the better we'll get to know you. This is a great chance for you to build your reputation with us. As you work with us, we'll get to know how you handle problems that come up, how you assess situations, and how dependable you are. Knowing that you're realistic and reasonable will make it easier for us to work with you when it comes to making decisions about your child. We'll be more likely to keep the lines of communication open, which means more information for you and more chances for us to work as a team to solve problems while they're still small. The time you spend building your reputation with us will definitely pay off.

Your child's age will have a lot to do with the type of volunteer opportunities available at his school. One of the main functions of preschool is to get children to operate independently of their parents, so there may not be many opportunities to volunteer in the classroom. But there are still parties to be planned, supplies to be collected, and field trips that require chaperones.

Elementary schools need classroom volunteers, people to run special events, chaperones, room moms and dads, and people to do prep work for teachers. At the junior high and high school levels, a big priority is again to get children to be more independent, so parents aren't typically allowed in classrooms. But chaperones are still needed, as are volunteers to distribute and collect books, run fundraisers, and man booster clubs.

No matter how old your child is, parent-teacher associations always need volunteers. A great way to get to know your school administrators is to get involved with your parent-teacher association (PTA) (or whatever this type of group is called at your school). You'll get to attend meetings with the people who run your school and get a chance to know them better. Sitting on site councils and getting involved with the school board also gives you access to administrators, at both at the school and the district levels.

By getting involved at your child's school, you'll also be providing an invaluable service to other students in special education. Because of the demands on special-needs families, their parents don't often volunteer. Parents of kids with special needs typically don't join the PTA or sit on councils or on the school board. That makes the needs of children in special education a little more invisible. Other parents are getting involved, and since they don't know much about special education, they don't always think about the needs of your kids. It's not intentional, and they're not discriminating against children with special needs. They just don't know. If you are there to speak up and work with those parents and school administrators, you'll be making your school a little more friendly for all students with special needs.

Volunteer at your child's school. We'll get a chance to earn your trust, and you'll get a chance to earn ours. The better we understand one another, the better we'll work together. All of us will benefit—especially your child.

CONCLUSION

I've spent the past decade talking to parents and teachers of children with autism, listening to their greatest fears, frustrations, and stories of success. I've heard the love in their voices when they speak about the children in their care, and I've heard the despair when they think they've failed them. I've seen them search for ways to help kids who had huge challenges, and I've seen their joy when they succeeded. I've helped dry the tears of both parents and teachers, when they felt they couldn't keep going another day. And I've seen them reach across the IEP table to hold the hand of someone who needed it, to assure them that, together, as a team, they would keep looking for answers.

Are there teachers out there who don't care about children? Are there parents who are so focused on "normalcy" that they can't work to help the child they have? Yes, but both are rare. Most commonly, people are doing the best they can in very difficult situations, with not enough information or support, but with the certainty that if they mess this up, a child will pay the price.

That's what it all boils down to—our children. To help them, we have to operate as a team. That means trusting someone else and being trustworthy ourselves. We have to appreciate the intent behind other people's actions and respect their opinions, even if they're different from our own. This means forgiving mistakes, asking a lot of questions, and listening even more. It will take all of our courage and patience to do this. We need to be able to put ourselves in someone else's shoes long enough for us to see why they're doing what they're doing. We need to learn more and be willing to try something new. And, most importantly, we need to keep our focus on finding the best way to get our children the help they need.

I am not saying that the team is more important than the child. We don't brush his needs aside to "make nice" with everyone else in the IEP meeting. When we need to stand firm, we do. If we need a lawyer, we get one. But lawyers and lawsuits are only one tool in our possession, and they're a tool of last resort. We'd be foolish to try to build a house with only one tool, and we can't build an education for a child that way, either.

CONCLUSION

Raising and teaching children with autism are not easy. That's only because we care. If we were content to just feed them, get them through school, and then fling them out into the adult world, our lives wouldn't be so hard. If they had a difficult time, so what? Challenges? Behaviors? Not our problem. Pass the children right on through, with no muss or fuss, and then we don't have to deal with it. But, that's not how we are. We love our kids, and we will move heaven and earth to help them the best we can.

That determination is what gets us through the hard times, but it can be a double-edged sword. Used productively, it helps us focus our efforts on helping our children to the best of our abilities. However, too often it gets turned on other people who also care about our kids. We yell at our spouses, blame teachers, or avoid interacting with the students' parents. Instead of using our passion to support their efforts, we use it to drive them away.

It doesn't matter how much we want to help our children; we can't do everything on our own. We need each other. We have to work together. Only then can our children truly reach their potential.

ABOUT THE AUTHOR

Cassie Zupke is the mother of three wonderful teenaged children, who, between them, have mild autism, ADHD, and physical impairments. They are also chronic geeks, just like their parents.

When her children were young, Cassie could find no one who could explain to her what "high-functioning autism" was or how she could help her son make it through the school day. Five long, hard years later, she found a special-education teacher who knew why her son did what he did and could teach him to navigate the world better. Cassie decided she didn't want other parents and teachers to have to face the same frustrations and worries that she had.

Cassie founded Open Doors Now, a nonprofit education and support group for students with mild autism, their families, and educators, and she serves as its director. In the past 10 years, Open Doors Now has educated thousands of parents, teachers, administrators, and other professionals about autism and how it affects our children and young adults. Owing to the hard work and dedication of the incredible volunteers at Open Doors Now, hundreds of kids have found friends, learned a few social skills, and had a lot of fun.